Teach®
Yourself

Cognitive Behavioural Therapy

Christine Wilding

Hodder Education

338 Euston Road, London NW1 3BH.

Hodder Education is an Hachette UK company

First published in UK 2008 by Hodder Education

First published in US 2008 by The McGraw-Hill Companies, Inc.

This edition published 2012

Previously published as *Teach Yourself Cognitive Behavioural Therapy*

British Library Cataloguing in Publication Data: a catalogue record for this title
is available from the British Library.

Library of Congress Catalog Card Number: on file.

10 9 8 7 6 5 4 3 2 1

The publisher has used its best endeavours to ensure that any website addresses
referred to in this book are correct and active at the time of going to press.
However, the publisher and the author have no responsibility for the websites
and can make no guarantee that a site will remain live or that the content will
remain relevant, decent or appropriate.

The publisher has made every effort to mark as such all words which it believes
to be trademarks. The publisher should also like to make it clear that the
presence of a word in the book, whether marked or unmarked, in no way affects
its legal status as a trademark.

Every reasonable effort has been made by the publisher to trace the copyright
holders of material in this book. Any errors or omissions should be notified
in writing to the publisher, who will endeavour to rectify the situation for any
reprints and future editions.

Hachette UK's policy is to use papers that are natural, renewable and recyclable
products and made from wood grown in sustainable forests. The logging
and manufacturing processes are expected to conform to the environmental
regulations of the country of origin.

www.hoddereducation.co.uk

Cover image © Nikolai Sorokin - Fotolia

Typeset by Cenveo Publisher Services.

Printed and bound by CPI Group (UK) Ltd, Croydon, CR0 4YY

Contents

Introduction to Cognitive Behavioural Therapy

How can we best resolve our problems?

How often do you catch yourself mulling over a concern and coming to very negative conclusions about it? Perhaps, after some time, you discover that your ruminations were incorrect and that your concerns were neither accurate nor important, but at the time you may have felt either extremely anxious or very depressed. Perhaps you tackled your problem by discussing it with friends or family, listening to their views and getting a different perspective on things. Possibly this helped you to see your problems differently and to feel calmer and more balanced about them – or possibly a number of different opinions left you even more bewildered and uncertain. What is right for someone else isn't always right for you, so working things out for yourself is usually a better option. However, this can be easy to say but hard to do.

Many of us spend a great deal of time trying to discover how we can feel better about ourselves, others or the world around us. We believe that if we can only get our lives into better shape, onto a more even keel or with increased personal or professional security, all will be well. Yet we miss a basic and obvious (when we think about it) premise: that the happiest and most well-adjusted among us are not always those who have achieved even semi-perfect lifestyles. They often have many difficulties in their lives or lead lives that we would not wish upon ourselves. So how can this be? How do we learn to feel good in spite of circumstance?

The power of inner resources

The answer is that we need to learn to tap into our inner resources. 'Feeling good' is right here, within you, because happiness, confidence and feeling good about yourself are emotions, not life events – not something you can touch, feel, purchase or pursue.

You are reading this book because you have an interest in 'being happier'. We (by which I mean 'you and I'; cognitive behavioural therapy (CBT) is a collaborative therapy so we will be working together all the way) won't try to create a specific definition of happiness here – which could easily take a book in itself – but simply accept the premise that you have your own definition of happiness and how it would give you a better sense of optimism and contentment. As you are considering CBT as a tool to help you (and, used wisely, it will), then probably – along with most of us – you would simply like to feel better within yourself, whether that might be as the result of a job promotion, a good personal relationship or better economic or financial circumstances. These are tangible concerns. Sometimes concerns are less tangible. They consist of an inability to stop worrying about things or to feel constantly depressed. Sometimes this can be because certain negative aspects of your past life won't seem to let you get over them and move forward, or it can be for what seems to you 'no reason at all' that you can quantify or explain.

Deciding on happiness

Eleanor Roosevelt, the wife of US President Franklin D. Roosevelt, was well-known for her succinct views on life. She famously once said: 'You can be just about as happy as you decide that you are going to be.'

Just so. Happiness is simply an emotion that we feel, dependent not on external events but on our thoughts about those events. Most of us know enough people who seem able to smile consistently through adversity to acknowledge the truth of this. But if we struggle with this idea and would love to overcome our own negativities, how do we proceed?

Cognitive behavioural therapy will help you. As its name suggests, this therapy focuses not on what happens to us but how we think about what happens to us and how we behave as a consequence. It then takes a look at whether our thinking and behaviours are improving our difficulties or maintaining them.

CBT does sound exceedingly simple, and many people dismiss it as 'just common sense'. But if it *were* just common sense, then no one would suffer from anxiety or low moods as they would be easily able to put things right themselves. CBT is like an interested detective. If things don't seem to get better for you even though you are applying lots of 'common-sense' solutions, CBT helps you to look for something else that is outside your own awareness at present. In a sense, it expands your awareness to embrace new thinking and new actions that don't always seem clear and obvious at the start but which can be life-changing once mastered. In doing so, CBT teaches you new life skills to achieve this.

This book will teach you these skills.

Because I suspect that most readers will be those with a general curiosity rather than specialists or academics, this book is written in what I hope is an easy-to-understand way. 'Layman's language' rather than psychological terms and jargon will be the style of writing and presentation. You will not get lost in 'in-depth findings' and research (except where I feel the research is dynamic enough to prove a point you might otherwise miss). You are going to learn some good, solid basic skills that I hope will stay with you forever. This book is designed to help those of you with real, chronic problems of worry and low mood, even despair. It is also designed to teach life skills that will make your life richer than it is now, even if it is OK at the moment.

Structured learning

The chapters are placed in a specific order so that what you learn in one chapter is summarized at the end of it and a short explanation is given of how this leads on to what you will learn in the following chapter. In this way the book is rather like a course or a class you might take.

Of course, you can dip in and out if you prefer, but the real benefit will come from starting at Chapter 1 and working through, a chapter at a time, so that you can consistently build on your skills. If this sounds rather like hard work, why not read the book through initially without undertaking any of the exercises and tasks. Get an idea of whether it all seems helpful and interesting, then go back to the beginning and get fully involved in acquiring the skills.

CBT as a therapy is very (very) precise. Working with vagaries, grasshoppering around, rambling at length – none of these things work well alongside CBT therapy; you will understand why as the book develops. To help this precision, you will be asked to write many things down so do have a good quality record system to hand. This might be your laptop, iPad or other electronic device or, if you prefer good old-fashioned pen and paper, ensure that you have a good quality notebook (not scraps of paper that may get lost or have a shopping list written on the back!) as you will need to refer back constantly to what you have written earlier in order to build on your learning. (I shall refer to this throughout as 'your workbook'.)

One comment made by a client on his first visit to me after reading a little bit about CBT in advance was that, 'It looked rather mechanical and just a lot of form-filling'. I understand what he meant – but *do* be assured that this isn't the case at all. Relentlessly filling in forms and trying to dredge up thoughts and feelings to pour into the chart columns given, simply because you are due to show them to your therapist the next day (or because this book says that you should) – rather than because you see any special virtue in undertaking the tasks – *is* very mechanical and won't get you very far.

This approach becomes rather like the drudgery of school homework. (In fact, CBT therapists actually call between-sessions exercises 'homework'). I have thus tried to keep the 'form filling' to a minimum and, even when there are charts and tables on the page, you are always given the opportunity of developing a method of recording things that seems pertinent and sensible to you. Good CBT should always work with you to find what suits you best and how you can be motivated and empowered to get the best results in your own particular way. This will only happen if you understand what you are doing and can see results from it. Ensure that you understand the purpose of what you are doing and why. If you don't 'get it', don't do it. It will be a waste of time. Go back over what you have read and see if you can glean more meaning from it, or conduct a brief experiment to try it out just once or twice and see whether a light comes on after the event, even though you didn't think it would before trying.

To help you become involved in constructing ways of learning that you feel comfortable with, I have tried to concentrate on giving you things to do that will expand your awareness and help you to think and see things differently as well as to try out different things and be curious about the results.

RATING YOUR EFFORT LEVELS FOR GOOD RESULTS

There is one proviso, however. When I work with clients I ask them to rate (very simply, from 1 to 10) the effort level they have put into the work they have done. If clients are consistently rating their effort as only 3 or 4, we look seriously at what is going wrong. It might be that the task isn't understandable or achievable, or it might be that the client thinks they can get by just 'winging it' and rushing through something just before their session.

I would like you to take up this rating system yourself. At the end of each chapter you will have this opportunity. Only when you can give yourself 8s and 9s will you have truly understood the material and be making good progress. So don't just 'wing it'!

You will almost certainly have come across the saying, 'Men are disturbed not by things, but by the view which they take of those things' (Epictetus (AD50–120; Greek philosopher). Most of us already appreciate this but it is the 'how do I do it?' that CBT addresses. Don't worry even if you are consumed by such ideas as:

▶ I cannot get rid of my negative thinking, no matter how hard I try.

▶ These aren't just negative thoughts, they are facts and truths. Pretending they are not won't change things.

▶ Nothing I do makes me feel any better.

These are common thoughts that many of us recognize, but the great thing about CBT is that it can weaken and eliminate even the strongest negative beliefs. The purpose of this book is to help you to learn the skills and techniques that will achieve this.

You will be amazed by how CBT can help you.

A general understanding of CBT

Before we start working on the particular skills and techniques of CBT, it would be helpful for you to have some idea of the concepts underlying the therapy and why it is currently regarded as the treatment of choice for achieving good mental health and well-being. You may think that CBT sounds a very simple and straightforward therapy – just 'common sense'. Up to a point this is true, but the purpose of CBT is to discover why, if solutions seem clear and obvious, our emotional difficulties don't go away. Why, despite all our best efforts, are we still stuck in the mud of depression, anxiety, stress and/or a variety of other frustrating 'feel bad' problems? This chapter will give you an answer.

The basic premise of CBT

Here's a thought:

> 'I've spent some hard-earned cash on this book but I'm really not sure that a book can help me with my problems.'

And what this thought might mean to you:

> 'Like so many things, I will probably start off enthusiastically and then lose motivation.'

Which could make you feel:

> Rather downhearted and depressed.

So what will you do?

> 'Well, give it a go but if I don't see quick results I'll ditch it.'

And what might the outcome be?

> 'Yet another book at the back of the bookshelf and the same old worries and problems whirling around in my head unresolved.'

This example demonstrates the premise of CBT – that what you think (and the personal meaning of those thoughts to you) will affect how you feel and what you do. I have made the first example a negative one since, if you are reading this book, you probably suffer from pessimistic thinking and are interested in learning how to do something about it.

Let's start again but with a different way of thinking:

'I've spent some hard-earned cash on this book but I'm really not sure that a book can help me with my problems.'

And what this thought might mean to you:

'I haven't spent a lot and, looking through it, it seems like easy reading with possibilities, so I'll take the positive view that it will help me rather than dismiss it without giving it a shot.'

Which could make you feel:

At least a little energized and motivated.

So what will you do?

'Rather than bite off more than I can chew and then give up on the book, I'll try a "little and often"' approach – just a few minutes a day or a chapter a week – and make sure I tackle the exercises rather than skipping over them.'

And what might the outcome be?

'While that is an unknown quantity there is a good chance that I will pick up a few ideas for generating more positivity in my life and if I really enjoy the concepts I am practising, it could be quite life-changing.'

AN ALTERNATIVE VIEW
Well, that's better! Nothing much has changed – the same book has been purchased for the same reasons – but the thinking and behaviour in the second example is more likely to give a positive, constructive outcome.

In essence, this is the basic premise of CBT:

> What you think
> (the Cognitive part)
>
> ↓
>
> determines how you feel (physically and emotionally)
>
> ↓
>
> which affects what you do
> (the Behavioural part)

Cognitions are your thoughts and the emotional effects they have on you; so 'cognitive' describes something relating to 'the mental action or process of acquiring knowledge and understanding through thought, experience, and the senses'.

The meaning of 'behavioural' is self-evident; 'behaviour' is the way in which an animal or person behaves in response to a particular situation or stimulus.

Let's try something that will help to give you a better idea of the effect of cognitions.

Remember this

Remember that you will need to have a notepad and pen, or your laptop, iPad or other electronic device, beside you when doing any exercises in this book. You won't have the same depth of recall and understanding if you try to do the exercises in your head; there will be too many other things going on in your brain so these thoughts and ideas won't stand out and 'stick'.

Think of a situation recently where things didn't go so well for you. Perhaps you made a mistake at work, had a disagreement with someone, burnt the dinner? Write down what you can recall of the thoughts you had about this at the time. These might have been along the lines of 'I'm hopeless at my job', 'No one ever sees my side of things' or 'I can't cook for toffee'.

How did these thoughts make you feel? Happy and confident or frustrated, upset or depressed? What about the physiology – did you feel energized by these thoughts or drained and lethargic?

And what did you do as a result? Write down your reactions to your thoughts about these events.

Now move on to thinking of a situation that was a happy one. Perhaps you achieved something you had been working towards, received an unexpected compliment or simply enjoyed a social event. Again, write down your thoughts about this situation as well as you can recall them. Perhaps you decided that you were quite smart to have achieved your goal, or a more amusing person than you had thought you were? Perhaps you simply thought how good life was generally when you were surrounded by friends?

How did these thoughts make you feel? Depressed and unhappy or elated and cheerful? Again, how did you feel physically – tired or energized? Write down any resulting behaviour(s) you can recall.

What connection can you make here between thoughts, feelings and actions?

Understanding the connections

When you take a close look at your thinking it becomes easier to see that if your thoughts are negative, how you *feel* will also be negative. You might also notice unpleasant physical symptoms (shortness of breath or panicky feelings or tiredness) and you may have reacted negatively as well.

However, if you had positive, upbeat thoughts about an event, it would be almost impossible to imagine that you felt anything other than cheerful, happy and physically energized, and exhibited positive behaviours (which might simply be laughing and smiling rather than scowling and grouching).

In other words, how you felt about the event depended on your view of the event rather than the event itself.

This can be shown in simple graphical terms.

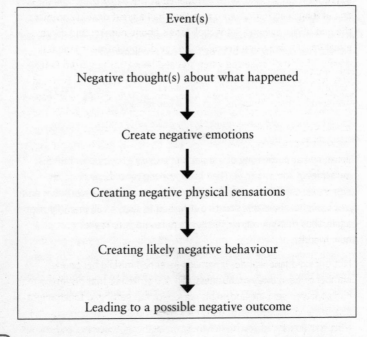

Event(s)

Negative thought(s) about what happened

Create negative emotions

Creating negative physical sensations

Creating likely negative behaviour

Leading to a possible negative outcome

Key idea

At its simplest, this is the premise of CBT. What you think decides how you feel and how you react. Of course, our thoughts are rarely the only predictors of outcomes, but they do play a very important role in deciding whether we feel happy or sad, up or down.

EMOTIONS HAVE A STRONG EFFECT ON US

Intriguingly, our thoughts alone don't affect us very much. Think about it for a moment: what affects us the most? It is the feelings that our thoughts engender that have the most power over us. It is, therefore, the fusion of thoughts and emotions that shapes our responses and reactions, which in turn may decide outcomes.

Case study

Jane met Peter at a party given by a friend who thought that they might hit it off. Indeed, once introduced at the party, they talked easily and at length and discovered that they had a great deal in common. At the end of the evening Peter took Jane's phone number and expressed a real interest in seeing her again. So the disappointment Jane felt a week after their meeting when she had heard nothing from Peter was acute. In Jane's mind, it became clear to her that Peter had had a rethink. Going over the evening again and again in detail, Jane realized that she had talked far too much, and had appeared silly, girlish and too obvious in her attraction to Peter. How could he possibly have been interested in someone like her? He was obviously just being polite in taking her number, embarrassed because their mutual friend had encouraged him to do so. The more Jane thought about this, the more depressed she became. She began to think of herself as worthless and unlovable, and resolved not to put herself in such a vulnerable position again, thus missing out on further opportunities to make new friends.

Not once did Jane wonder if perhaps Peter had mislaid her phone number or been away on business. It didn't strike her that his interest had appeared genuine and so his reason for not getting in touch might also be genuine. Jane's emotions took over and the more unhappy she became, the more negative her thoughts became. A vicious cycle of unhappiness.

Three days later, Peter did ring. He'd had the 'flu and was only just recovering, he said. By this time, Jane's own 'He never really liked me' convictions were foremost in her mind and she construed Peter's call as nothing more than a courtesy. Peter, deterred by Jane's negative 'vibes', simply apologized again and ended the call.

Can you see how Jane's thinking, rather than Peter's inaction, had led to her feelings of depression and worthlessness? What a shame. Jane had caused her confidence to drop so badly through a cycle of negative thinking that a potential relationship never came to fruition. Can you see how Jane's thinking drove her emotions? And how Jane's emotions drove her thinking? Strong connections: keep them in mind.

CBT to the rescue

The idea of resolving problems by talking about them, rather than by taking medications, is relatively new. In the late 19th century, Sigmund Freud developed psychoanalytical therapy, which emphasized the role of unresolved conflicts from childhood in determining how we thought and felt as adults. This was followed in the 1950s by behavioural therapy, which worked on the principle that psychological problems were caused by faulty learning and could be resolved by teaching people to change or modify their behaviours to achieve more positive results. Then, in the 1960s, the American psychiatrist Aaron Beck added a cognitive component that proved a powerful success in giving people a more balanced and optimistic outlook. He had noticed that people he worked with seemed more concerned with their current thoughts, such as, 'I wonder if I'm saying the right sort of thing?', 'Perhaps I'm coming across as a rather selfish person', than they were in the stories from their past that they were relating. In effect, the client would be saying one thing but thinking another, and the emotions they were feeling were related to their conscious mind and the 'here and now' rather than their tales of long ago.

Beck discovered that many of his clients had such thoughts quite regularly in their interactions with other people. So he started working with his clients' conscious and current thought processes and discovered that by helping the client to adjust these thoughts positively, they began to feel very much better without especially touching on their past histories.

Beck called this therapy cognitive therapy, and subsequently cognitive behavioural therapy, based on his realization that what his clients thought not only affected how they felt but also how they behaved. It became clear to Beck that if he could find ways of helping people view things differently – in a more balanced, rather than overly pessimistic or anxious, way – then their emotions might also change in line with a more optimistic thinking style and lead as well to more positive reactions.

The current therapy of choice

One reason for CBT's surge in popularity is that it has been the first talking therapy that has stood the test of scientific audit. CBT has proved its efficacy by its ability to be empirically measured.

Since its development in the 1960s, cognitive theory has been widely researched – Beck himself set up the Institute for Cognitive Therapy and Research in Pennsylvania – and treatment protocols have been developed to treat most psychological disorders. Results have been monitored and outcomes evaluated. These audited outcome records prove that the therapy has a positive effect on the majority of those who learn how to use it to cope with their life problems.

Key idea

I mention the points above to give you confidence in CBT. As you practise its skills you can do so in the knowledge that these are all proven techniques, shown time after time to provide positive outcomes, rather than merely fashionable ideas that may or may not work. So this is a well-researched and validated therapy that you can benefit from yourself.

Remember this

CBT is sometimes criticized for not placing more emphasis on the past. Although our childhoods or earlier life experiences can have a great influence on how we think and feel, research shows that many of those whose childhoods were traumatized develop into stable grown-ups, while some adults with idyllic upbringings develop psychological problems. CBT accounts for this difference by looking at how an individual's current thinking style may have developed more from faulty perceptions than from actual events.

CBT *is* interested in a client's past, but only in order to discover how beliefs and assumptions that are unhelpful in the present have developed. For example, if elements of your childhood had left you with the belief that you were never good enough, that may explain why, for instance, you never apply for promotion at work, or always bail out of emotional relationships. By finding out clients' beliefs about themselves, CBT can help them to check the present accuracy of such beliefs and adjust their thinking to embrace more helpful and appropriate beliefs for the present and the future.

Talking the talk

The present generation is much more open about expressing how we feel and discussing our emotions. The old 'stiff upper lip' approach that used to hold sway has given way to the idea that talking things through when things go wrong emotionally is helpful and widely regarded as sensible.

CBT fits the bill here exactly. Unlike insight-based therapies such as psychodynamic therapy, CBT is a solution-focused, short-term therapy, and because it involves the client in doing a great deal of work themselves, results are quick, effective and lasting.

I (and others) have always referred to CBT as the psychology of common sense. People understand it. However, its purpose isn't just to point out the obvious, but rather to enquire of you: 'If the solution is obvious (even if unpalatable), why is your problem still with you? What is it that is preventing you from resolving it yourself?' This is where the therapy starts – by helping us to work out just why we cannot resolve our problems: what perceived obstacles are preventing us from doing so and how can we remove those obstacles. Also, common sense doesn't always provide all the answers. For example, if someone has a fear of AIDS, and the fear doesn't go away no matter how many medical checks and reassurances they have, something more than common sense is required to work out what is going on and to find a solution. CBT can achieve this.

The connection between thoughts and emotions, and the idea that, in most instances (though not all), it is our thinking that decides our emotions, places huge value on working with cognitions in order to manage emotions. If adjusting our thinking failed to alter our emotional reactions, CBT would have been binned as a therapy process.

What problems does CBT help?

The applications of CBT extend far beyond those described in this book. Eating disorders, relationship problems, substance misuse, bipolar disorder, agoraphobia, chronic fatigue syndrome, sexual problems and psychosis, borderline personality disorder, avoidant personality disorder, paranoia and schizophrenia are all psychological problems that respond well to CBT. However, it would be wrong to suggest that overcoming such problems could be achieved just by reading a book. Where problems are severe and chronic, professional help will be required to overcome them.

Try it now

Practise the earlier exercise of finding an event and recalling what happened, your thoughts about what happened, how you felt and what you did. This will develop your understanding of the link between thoughts and feelings. Using the format given, go through it again and again, writing possibilities down in your workbook. Each time, identify what was going on, what you thought and how you felt.

Then reread this chapter, ensuring that it all makes sense to you before you go on to Chapter 2.

Focus points

* You now have some idea of the connection between thoughts, feelings and behaviour that is the basic principle from which CBT therapy has developed.

* Keep with you a constant awareness of these connections, so that it starts to make easy sense to you.

* The development of psychological therapy as a valid helping tool has grown apace since the advent of CBT. Once confined to the seriously ill in mental institutions, it has now become a popular choice for many people to deal with problems that relate as much to positive personal development as to adverse circumstances.

* While CBT is now used to help a wide variety of psychological problems, when these are severe and chronic, professional help is the way to overcome them.

* A real 'plus' of CBT is that it is easy to understand and makes sense to most people. Not only do they get better but they can understand why they are getting better, which in turn prevents the risk of relapse. CBT is an educational model teaching the client (or the reader) the life skills to become their own therapist.

Rate your effort (1–10) for the exercises you have tried in this chapter ......

Next step

Now that you have some idea of the aims of CBT, its background and development together with a small notion of the connection between thoughts, feelings and behaviours, we will move forward into CBT's practical skills, starting with an explanation of how to identify negative thoughts together with an understanding of how much they can hinder us and life outcomes.

2

Setting your goals

Before we talk further about the skills of CBT, it is important to emphasize that it is a very solution-focused therapy. It spends time working out what the problem is, what maintains the problem and what the solution to the problem might be. To achieve this, CBT has to work with goals and so it is important that you have set some goals for yourself before you start using CBT's skills and techniques.

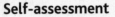

? Self-assessment

1 Am I someone who regularly sets goals for myself?

2 Do I tend to achieve the goals that I set?

3 What do I want to achieve from reading this book?

4 How do I think this book will help me to reach this goal?

5 Do I have a definite plan or simply a vague idea?

When you have answered these questions, you will have given yourself a good general idea of whether or not you work in a goal-oriented way (questions 1 and 2) and if so, whether you are planning or setting goals for your CBT reading and learning (questions 3–5).

If you have answered the questions positively and now have a good structure, feel free to skip to this chapter. However, I suspect it is more likely that some discussion about goal-setting may be helpful to you. Once you are more familiar with this idea, set yourself small goals for each chapter of this book. Some chapters will be more important to you than others; where they are important to you, ask yourself what you would like to have learned by the end of the chapter, or read the chapter through and if you cannot envisage clearly what you feel you could have achieved, go through the chapter again until you gain what you want from it.

What does 'having a goal' mean?

'Would you tell me, please, which way I ought to go from here?'

'That depends a good deal on where you want to get to,' said the Cat.

'I don't much care where – ' said Alice.

'Then it doesn't matter which way you go,' said the Cat.

Lewis Carroll, *Alice's Adventures in Wonderland*

This extract from Lewis Carroll's famous story underlines the importance of knowing where you want to go before you set off down any path.

A goal refers to what you are totally committed to achieving. Think long and hard about what it is that you really wish to achieve – perhaps within a month, three months, six months or a year's time – and be honest with yourself about this.

As a general rule, it's inadvisable to set goals beyond a year because your priorities may change; also, setting very long-term goals makes them seem an impossibly long way off. By keeping goals closer, they will appear as more than just a distant dream.

OBJECTIVES: PAVING THE WAY TOWARDS YOUR GOALS

Objectives are the stepping stones which guide you to achieving your goals. They must be verifiable in some way, whether that's statistically – 'the more I do this, the better I get at it' – or by some other achievable concept such as getting the job or relationship that you want. It's crucial that your objectives lead you logically towards your goal and are quantifiable.

The great thing is that after each objective is achieved, you are rewarded with a warm feeling of satisfaction and increased confidence.

Key idea

As with your goals, your objectives should be well thought-out. The time you take to draw up your goals and objectives will ultimately ensure that they are accurate, realistic and flexible – and that they are right for you.

UPDATING YOUR GOALS AND OBJECTIVES

When you've achieved your goal or goals (as a result of achieving all the objectives along the way), it will be time to set a new goal, and so the process starts all over again. However, this doesn't mean that you have to be constantly setting challenging goals. It could be as simple as just maintaining what you have achieved so far.

USING YOUR UNDERSTANDING OF WHERE YOU ARE NOW TO SET NEW GOALS FOR YOURSELF

'What do I want to achieve?' or 'How do I want things to be different?' are good basic questions in goal-setting.

Remember this

Stephen Covey, author of *The Seven Habits of Highly Effective People*, makes a brief but important statement when he says, 'Begin with the end in mind'.

This section of the book is to help you work out what is important enough to you for you to work on yourself.

Key idea

Sometimes we describe our goals in a negative way – knowing what we don't want can be easier to describe than knowing what we do want. This isn't very helpful, in the same way that setting unachievable goals which can only lead to failure and disappointment. So goal-setting is more than writing a few ideas on a piece of paper. It is a skill that is vital to setting you off on the right track.

Case study

Mary's daughter was getting married and her excitement was palpable. Mary wanted to be sure that this was the best day of her daughter's life and to share this joy with her fully. Plans started to be made, dates were set, invitation lists drawn. Everything was moving forward nicely except one thing: Mary's weight. Always a large woman, the pounds seemed to be piling on now and Mary's attempts to stem the tide had little effect. Cutting out sugar and hoping that would do it hadn't made much difference. So Mary decided on a drastic step – she would have a week of liquids only. This lasted until the evening of the first day, when a chocolate bar became too alluring to be dismissed and everything went to pot. Then someone suggested exercise would make a difference – but what to do? Mary tried skipping, jogging (for about two minutes, until she became breathless) and running up and down stairs, which was all very dull and nearly caused a sprained ankle. A cabbage soup diet followed, then one that involved only eating protein and nothing else, but these diets were all so hard to follow that the results were negligible. Mary was making so much effort but nothing was changing. Where was Mary going wrong? The answer was given by the slimming club she finally attended at a friend's suggestion. Until then Mary had no *specific* goals, just wild hopes combined with a willingness to try, but not especially stick with, anything. But after four weeks at the club (and with three weeks to the wedding day) Mary had shed 11 pounds! The reason for this success was simple. The slimming club made Mary define her goals very exactly.

* How much weight did she want to lose overall?
* When did she want to lose it by?
* What did this mean her weekly goal would be?
* Was this realistically achievable or should it be adjusted?
* What choice of diet would she undertake?
* How would she shop for the food she would need?
* When would she do it?
* How would she handle cravings?

For the first time, Mary had written down objectives and goals. She had lots of small, manageable and achievable steps to take that gave her optimism and success, and a target that got closer and closer and was achievable.

As Mary learned, the more specific your goals are, the more likely you are to achieve them.

Key idea

Researchers in the US tracked a group of college students over 30 years. They discovered that those who had written down their goals (just 3 per cent) had succeeded in achieving them. A further 58 per cent had goals in their heads as they left college, and they had far less success. The remainder of students left college without any goals in mind, and most of any good fortune they achieved in the following 30 years was down more to good luck than any planning. So write your goals down and stick with them!

SUCCESS BREEDS SUCCESS

In the US in the 1960s, the advertising industry boomed and being a salesman was seen as a good way to make money. However, most companies set the bar high for achieving bonuses from good sales figures, and if you did achieve the target it was raised for the next round of sales. In the end, this could become demoralizing and many salespeople gave up. The computer industry was also booming at this time, and IBM became the IT industry's giant of the era, with excellent profits from selling computers in vast numbers. Investigating why IBM salespeople were so successful, researchers found that IBM set *easy* targets for their salespeople rather than targets that were difficult to reach and so most of their salespeople achieved their targets. IBM had hired psychologists to define optimum motivational goals for their salespeople and it was discovered that if the targets were achievable the salespeople became very confident and motivated (unlike their demotivated cousins in rival companies) and went out and sold even more computers.

So the lesson here is: make your targets achievable. You will feel a surge of success when you reach them and this will encourage you to continue. Learn from the IBM psychologists of the 1960s!

The characteristics of good goal-setting

Achievable goals have a set of characteristics that make them so. These characteristics include the following.

▶ Ensure that your goals are flexible. Think of your goal(s) as a piece of plasticine whose shape you can mould as you gather more information and perhaps prefer a new direction. Don't set your goals in stone. Good goals have built-in flexibility so they can be adjusted as you, your life and your personal desires change. What you are doing now is just a start.

▶ When you are setting goals, think about them in terms of short-, medium- and long-term goals. Set yourself short-term goals that you could reasonably achieve within, say, a week or even a day, medium-term goals which could be achieved within a month or two, and long-term goals which you might work on long afterwards, especially emphasizing positive changes and targets for personal growth.

THE SMART MODEL

There is a well-known model for goal-setting that is taught on business courses worldwide. It is just as useful for you when setting your own goals. (If you are already well versed in the SMART model, then do move on.)

SMART stands for:

▶ S = Specific

▶ M = Measurable

▶ A = Attainable

▶ R = Realistic

▶ T = Timely

Any goals you set should be able to meet each of the above criteria.

▶ **Being specific**

Goals should be straightforward and emphasize what you want to happen. Specifics help us to focus our efforts and clearly define what we are going to do.

Specific is the what, why and how of the SMART model.

▶ what are you going to do?

▶ why is this important to do it at this time?

▶ how are you going to do it? (By using CBT skills in this case.)

Ensure the goal you set is very specific, clear and easy. Instead of setting a goal to lose weight or be healthier, set a specific goal to lose 2 cm off your waistline or to walk 5 miles at an aerobically challenging pace.

▶ **If you can't measure it, you can't manage it**

Choose a goal with measurable progress, so you can see the change occur. How will you see when you reach your goal? Be specific! 'I want to read at least five classic novels by the end of November' shows a specific target to be measured. 'I want to be a good reader' is not as measurable.

▶ Can I attain it?

When you identify goals that are most important to you, you begin to work out ways you can achieve them. You develop the attitudes, abilities and skills to reach them. You may begin to see previously overlooked opportunities that bring you closer to the achievement of your goals.

You probably won't commit to achieving goals you've set that are too far out of your reach. Although you may start with the best of intentions, the knowledge that it's too much for you means your subconscious will keep reminding you of this fact and will stop you from even giving it your best shot.

▶ Is the goal realistic?

Realistic in this sense means what you are most likely to be able to stick with in the long term. Deciding never to eat cakes or sweets again, for example, is very unlikely to succeed. A more realistic goal might be to reduce your consumption of these things.

▶ What is my time frame?

Achieving your goal(s) within a specific time frame is vital. If you don't do this, your commitment will be vague. Nothing tends to happen if you know you can start and finish at any time and there is no urgency to act. However, as already mentioned, make your time frame realistic. All your goals must have at least some chance of success for you to pursue them. For example, if I asked you to join a marathon run with me next Monday you would almost certainly say 'no' (unless you were already in the final stages of training for a marathon). However, if I asked you to run a marathon with me in a year's time, you might say 'yes' as you would have enough time to prepare. This is where time frames and realism coincide.

Key idea

When you identify areas that are currently causing you problems and that could be improved, the next step is to log them as a *goal list* of issues to work on.

How to begin working out your goals

While the SMART model is very useful for assessing the efficacy of your goals, before you reach that stage you need to think about what your goals will be.

Key idea

Once you have worked through these criteria you will now have quite a list of things that you would like to be different. These are now your goals.

YOUR NEXT STEP

Once you have drawn up a list of goals it is vital to prioritize them. You are unlikely to be able to achieve everything you are hoping for at once and it is important not to jump back and forth from one thing to another. A good way to prioritize things is to give them each a value rating. Someone I knew had a new Porsche at the top of his list and spending more time with his family at around number five. However, once he had given honest ratings to their value to him, he found that his car dropped down the list and spending more time with his family rose to the top.

Try it now

Prioritize your goals. Which is the most important to you, and why? A good question to ask yourself can be, 'Which goal would I sacrifice the others for?'. The answer can certainly adjust your original priorities.

WHERE DO I START?

Most people assume that you should start at the top of your list of priorities, but this is not always the case. Using your SMART model, look at the time element. Is there an urgency to any of the goals? Then that is where you start. However, where time is not a critical factor, give your goals a further rating on a spectrum from 'hardest to achieve' to 'easiest to achieve'.

The issue of which goals to tackle first will be resolved by the easy/hard ratings you give them. It is helpful if initially you tackle easier goals and those where change is likely to occur quite rapidly, in order to give yourself hope and confidence. But there is nothing remotely wrong in doing things the other way around, and starting with the hardest thing on the list. If you succeed there, then all else suddenly becomes easy. However, bear in mind the warning earlier in this chapter about setting oneself up for failure if you try to achieve too much too soon, and ask yourself how you would be able to handle that if you don't go for the more 'sure fire' success of getting easier goals off the list first.

Key idea

Some goals need to be tackled urgently, to avoid a crisis. Others would bring immediate improvement to your life. If any of your goals fall into one of these categories, decide which is more important to you and, ignoring other factors, place it at the top of your goal list.

AN IMPORTANT DISTINCTION

There are further decisions you can make about your goals that will help you decide what approach to take: whether you want to work cognitively, or behaviourally, or both. This can then be built into your plan of action.

Try it now

Now to divide your goals into two sub-sections. Look through them all and consider the following.

* Which of these goals can only be achieved by my doing something?
* Which of these goals might be achieved if I thought differently about them?

For example, if you find it difficult to get on with your boss at work, you have the choice of discussing it with him or her, or handing in your notice – or you could decide to work on not allowing him to continue to 'get' to you. You can decide what to set as your goal from the various options. However, for example, if you feel frustrated by the fact that you are not very tall, your goal will have to be the second option of coming to terms with it.

When you write your goals down, it can be most helpful to do so in the form of a chart. This will give you greater clarity than a simple list. You can develop your own chart, but below is an example that you might consider.

Main goal	Time frame	Mini goals	Time frame	Note your action achieved or revised
To work through this book and apply my learning to my personal situation(s).	6 months	To work on one chapter at a time and have confidence in my understanding before I move on.	1 chapter a week	
To identify specific positive changes I wish to make to my life.	Immediately	To identify the small steps I can make towards achieving my main goal(s).	4 weeks	

Use your goal plan to work out your needs, and list the action you need to take *very specifically* in order to achieve them. For example, saying 'To lose weight' is too vague – how much, by when, and exactly how do you plan to do it?

Remember this

Goals need to be flexible. As you develop strategies for meeting your goals, you may find that you wish to change them. Remember, a flexible goal is like a piece of plasticine that you can mould and change as you develop and learn.

Always remember: achieving your goals depends on your ability to take action

Focus points

* Set your goals before you start to learn new skills and techniques.
* Make sure that you set your goals out clearly and specifically – vague goals will achieve nothing as they are too hard to quantify.
* Goal-setting can be time-consuming. Be prepared to spend some time on it and don't rush through it. In therapy terms, it is easily possible to spend a whole session of time simply working on goals and putting a structure in place for them.
* Review your goals constantly. Our goals can change as our circumstances (or desires) change, and it is fine to restructure them at any point. They are cast in plasticine, not concrete.
* When you have achieved your goals, always set new ones, even if this is simply the maintenance of the goal(s) you have achieved so far. Don't allow yourself to lose the gains you have made.

Rate your effort (1–10) for the exercises you have tried in this chapter ......

Next step

Now that you have set your goals, in Chapter 3 we will begin to look seriously at the skills and techniques you need to start using in order to achieve them. We look in more detail at the thoughts that may be unhelpful to you, that may not be true (even though you believe them) and how to begin replacing these thoughts with more helpful and optimistic ones.

Also, from Chapter 3 onwards, chapter goals will be set as part of the process of learning to develop specific goals for moving forward. It will be up to you to make sure that you achieve them!

Identifying your problems

You can only set problem-solving goals if you know what the problems are. By the end of this chapter you should be able to:

▶ *identify your problems by examining thoughts and feelings*

▶ *understand that your problems may not necessarily arise from events but from your thoughts and feelings about those events.*

Self-assessment

1 Do you often think that you know what others are thinking, especially about you?

2 Do you find yourself expecting disaster? For example, 'something is sure to go wrong'.

3 Do you personalize general comments? For example, you relate a passing remark on short hairstyles or the benefits of going to the gym to criticism of your own short hair or lack of fitness?

4 Do your generalize specific incidents? For example, if someone treats you unfairly, do you decide that you are unlikeable?

5 Do you sometimes blame others for your own thoughts or actions? For example, 'If he hadn't done what he did, I wouldn't have reacted that way'.

A 'yes' to any (or all) of these questions makes you fairly normal – we all do these things – but nonetheless shows that your thinking is skewed and might account for any life difficulties you are experiencing.

We all have many thoughts going round in our heads all the time. In her seminal book *Feel the Fear and Do It Anyway*, Susan Jeffers refers to these as our 'chatterbox'. One of my clients beautifully described this constant brain activity as a 'sort of Google search engine, running relentlessly in the background, looking for something new to ponder on'. Eckhart Tolle, in *The Power of Now*, refers to: 'the brain's noise-making activity that we refer to as thinking'. All good descriptions of the enormous mass of thoughts that seem to preoccupy us most of the time.

There are three broad categories of thoughts.

▶ Some may be positive and/or constructive – looking forward to an event, thinking about something good that happened at work or a new friend you have made.

▶ Many others will be neutral thoughts – acknowledging the day's events and making minor decisions about what to have for dinner, which television programme to watch, whether to phone a friend or not.

▶ These two categories of thinking don't have the same impact on us as the third category: negative thoughts. Negative thoughts cause us to interpret ideas or events in a pessimistic way and can cause us to feel anxious or depressed. So these are the thoughts that we want to work on, either to eliminate them or to replace them with more balanced alternatives.

Negative automatic thoughts

In CBT we call negative thoughts 'automatic', or NATs (negative automatic thoughts) for short. This is because these thoughts pop into our heads without any help from us – they simply seem to be there – and they stay there, even when they are causing us great distress and we wish they would go away. They have a huge effect on the way you feel and what you are able to do. Negative thoughts such as 'I can't cope' or 'I feel terrible' make you feel more anxious and unhappy, and can themselves be a major cause of anxiety or depression. While some of these thoughts may be based on real events, a lot of them are simply guesses and assumptions.

When your initial thoughts are negative, your assumptions are also likely to be negative, compounding the thinking error and making the problem worse. These are your *negative automatic thoughts,* usually unrealistically pessimistic and coming from nowhere to 'automatically' enter your mind. It feels as though someone is chattering away in your head or that there is a radio that you cannot turn off. Even worse, if we try to block them out they persist even more strongly.

Try it now

Picture a pink flamingo. A pretty, elegant bird that probably fills your mind with a rather pleasant picture. Now tell yourself that if you can go for one minute without thinking of a pink flamingo something really good will happen.

Are you ready?

What happens?

Now ask yourself how many times you thought about pink flamingos in the last week? So how often was that? If you didn't, why didn't you?

The answer, of course, is that you tried to block flamingos out of your mind when it was important that you did, yet this proved impossible. That which we resist, persists. When it doesn't matter whether we have a thought or not – when the thought has no meaning – it can simply come or not come, it really doesn't matter. Unless you had a special interest in flamingos or had just seen some in the zoo, they would not have entered your mind – until you instructed yourself to get them out of your mind, which no doubt conjured up hundreds of pink flamingos that refused to be removed.

Key idea

This is a very important lesson, as CBT is *not* (as many believe) about controlling your thinking and blocking out negative thoughts. You would have very little success with this; indeed, you may have tried it in the past, and found it is hard work and rarely works for long.

What *is* CBT about, then?

CBT is about taking a long, hard look at the *validity* of your thoughts, then re-evaluating them, offering yourself more rational, balanced and open-minded alternatives that will have a better place in your mind than faulty, negative, concrete-hard thoughts and beliefs.

So a major characteristic of NATs that we need to dispute is that they have *meaning* to us. 'If I think this it must be true.' 'If I think that then it will happen.'

Remember this

It is very important to remember that it is not the *thoughts* that unnerve us but the *meaning* we give to those thoughts, i.e. what we personally make of them.

Recognizing negative thoughts

One of the problems with recognizing negative thoughts is that they are very good at appearing, on the face of things, to be rational truths. Because of this we rarely question them and simply 'go along' with their chatter in our heads. Also, when asked to pinpoint what they are thinking that is causing them to feel sad or anxious, people will say something like, 'I'm really not thinking anything much' or 'Try as I might, I can't identify anything that is bothering me'. A reason for this can be that our emotions have taken over and we feel swamped by feelings – anxiety, panic, severe low mood. These emotions may also have a physical component – stomach churning, general tenseness, tiredness, etc. – so we tend to focus more on how we are feeling than what we are thinking.

THE FIRST STEP – AWARENESS

Simply becoming aware of these thoughts can help you to understand why your moods are negative, and this is a good first step towards learning to think in a more helpful, positive way. To help you achieve this awareness, it will help to be more familiar with what negative thoughts look like.

Frustratingly (and cleverly), negative thoughts tend to spring to mind without any effort from you, they are easy to believe (even though they're often not at all true) and they have a relentless way of staying with you the more you try to ditch them.

Try it now

Practising awareness is an excellent way to begin. As you go about your day, 'check in' with your thinking from time to time. Is your thinking in that moment optimistic and constructive or is it just endless rumination that serves no real purpose? Practise this regularly – don't try to examine or eliminate your thoughts at this stage, simply acknowledge that your 'chatterbox' is at work – and you will begin to have a real awareness of how time-wasting and negative a great deal of what passes through your mind is.

BEGINNING TO USE THIS NEW AWARENESS

Once you find negative thoughts and concepts easier to notice and identify you can begin to examine them. You can do this by writing them down in a structured way, the usual tool in CBT being a 'Thought Record'. We will develop the idea of Thought Records with you now, as they are one of the most helpful basic CBT tools for thought-challenging. The more you practise filling in Thought Records, the greater will become your awareness of your thoughts and your understanding of the effect they have on how you feel.

Try it now

To create a simple Thought Record, take a sheet of paper and divide it vertically into three columns and fill in the headings of each column

Event(s)	Thought(s)	Feelings/physical sensations
(What happened?)	(What went through my mind)	(How did I feel emotionally and what physical sensations did I notice?)

Now, using any recent event that you can think of, fill in the three columns. Doing this makes you 'notice' a lot more of what is actually going on; you begin to pay attention to thoughts and feelings that you had not overly noticed previously. This awareness is a first big step towards positive change.

Here's an example:

Event(s)	Thought(s)	Feelings/physical sensations
(What happened?)	(What went through my mind)	(How did I feel emotionally and what physical sensations did I notice?)
It's my birthday today and my husband hasn't mentioned it.	He's completely forgotten, which shows how little I mean to him now.	Disappointed, hurt, worthless. Heaviness in stomach.

BUT MY BRAIN IS SO FULL OF THOUGHTS...

We have hundreds of thoughts in our heads at any given time and sifting through them all could seem an enormous task. Some of these thoughts are important but many are not. Some make us feel good, others worry us. Gathering thoughts into groups can be a good start in helping you to weed out the useless ones.

Try it now

✻ Put your thinking cap on and write down any different types of thoughts you can think of.

✻ Why might it be helpful to know something of these different types of thoughts?

Did you have any of the following on your list?

▶ **Positive thoughts** make us feel good; for example, 'I'm excited about my holiday'. Thoughts like these make us feel happy, although we will rarely notice that the thought drives the feeling.

▶ **Neutral thoughts** are those which have no special effect on us; for example, 'Which dress shall I wear?', 'What's on TV tonight?'. These thoughts don't normally engender any emotion at all.

▶ **Evaluative thoughts** get us questioning things; for example, 'I wonder if I am likely to get the promotion I want?', 'Do these shoes look right with this dress?'. We may feel some slight flutter of anxiety over these but are unlikely to feel any extreme emotion.

▶ **Rational thoughts** are similar to evaluative thoughts; for example, 'I'm sure I've done the right thing, but if not, it won't be too serious'. Again, it is unlikely that we will experience any strong emotions with such thoughts.

▶ **Action-oriented thoughts** are very positive and usually of a problem-solving nature; for example, 'I'm determined to be best in my group', 'I'm not giving up, no matter how hopeless it seems'. The emotions from this type of thinking are usually optimism and confidence.

The reason it is important to have an understanding of all categories of thought is to enable us to notice more clearly those which are negative and not to waste our time on thoughts that don't especially affect us.

Again, it's all down to emotions. If we have thoughts that upset us, we need to work on these particular thoughts (unless we like being upset: most of us don't). All other thoughts can simply cruise past in the background, so don't waste your time with them.

Key idea

The way you think has an important effect on the way you feel and what you are able to do. Pessimistic, negative thoughts such as 'I can't cope' or 'I feel terrible' make you feel more anxious and unhappy, and can themselves be a major cause of any anxiety or low mood.

Remember this

Some of your negative thoughts may be based on reality, but some will probably be 'guesswork' and you may be jumping to conclusions that paint things blacker than they are. We call these *negative automatic thoughts* because they are unrealistically pessimistic and because they seem to come from nowhere and 'automatically' enter your mind.

Try it now

Use the table below (or make your own if you prefer not to write in the book) to think a bit more broadly about your initial thoughts. Note a couple of recent events (i.e. 'My boss didn't like my presentation'. 'My best friend forgot my birthday') about which you had negative thoughts (e.g. 'I'm going to get the sack soon'. 'My friend doesn't care about me'). Then critically ask yourself – is this a fact or just my way of looking at things?

Event	Initial thought	Fact or negative viewpoint?
It's my birthday today and my husband hasn't mentioned it.	He's completely forgotten, which shows how little I mean to him now.	Just a negative viewpoint.

Hopefully you will now be starting to be more discerning and critical of these 'truths' and realize that many 'facts' are simply assumptions.

We usually find it easy to spot when others are thinking in a negative, pessimistic way. Yet when it comes to our own thoughts, we nearly always think that they are rational and valid facts, however negative they are. It rarely occurs to us that we might suffer from what is called Negative Thinking Bias (which means that when we have a choice of thinking about something in a negative or a positive way, we veer to the negative way out of habit) or that these thoughts might be causing us to feel emotionally negative or even be tipping us into depression.

Try it now

You can use the same examples that you chose above if you wish, but the third column now asks you to develop a new 'take' on your initial thoughts of the event. This alternative thought should be a more optimistic, *though still realistic*, alternative. I emphasize 'realistic' as any alternative viewpoint that is very far away from your current one is likely to be totally unbelievable that it is pointless. If you feel that your work colleague undermined you, telling yourself that you were mistaken and they actually think you are great won't work. What might work is something along the lines of, 'Although I felt undermined by my colleague they were probably simply trying to describe their own point of view'. You might find yourself able to consider this alternative realistically (and feel a little better for doing so).

Here you go ......

Event	Negative thought	How else can I look at this?
It's my birthday today and my husband hasn't mentioned it.	He's completely forgotten, which shows how little I mean to him now	He might have a surprise up his sleeve that he hasn't mentioned yet or, even if he has forgotten, it's more likely to be absent-mindedness than lack of love.

MINI-SUMMARY

Here is a mini-summary of what you should be able to do now (to ensure you are not beginning to feel confused).

▶ You should have an awareness of periods of negative, unproductive thinking.

▶ You should be able to identify the negative emotions (at least generally) that these thoughts give rise to.

▶ You should be starting to appreciate that these thoughts are not (always) truths but can be assumptions that you should not let slip by without evaluation.

▶ As you evaluate your thinking more, you should be starting to notice that you feel a little better as a result.

'But my problems are real and tangible'

None of this is to say that you are not experiencing a time in your life when everything seems to go wrong and you simply feel stuck. Nonetheless, however real and horrendous your problems may be, you can still become more resilient in dealing with them through reacting to them differently.

Sometimes, identifying what is wrong in an exact way is extremely difficult. A common problem can be that of *not* being able to define exactly why you feel as you do.

Such problems are not as specific as, for example, financial or relationship worries, and tend be expressed in our heads in more general terms – such as feelings of isolation or 'hard-to-pinpoint-exactly' worries about the future.

A good first question to start with when trying to work things out is 'How would I like things to be and what is preventing this?'.

If you feel that life sucks or that you would like to feel differently about yourself, ask yourself in what way you would like things to be different and why this isn't happening. In other words, don't dwell on your problems (unproductive thinking); instead, become curious about what might be maintaining them (constructive thinking).

CONCEPTUALIZATION

CBT suggests that a great way to work out what exactly your problems are and what is maintaining them is by 'conceptualizing' them. This means taking all the things that are happening to you – events, thoughts, feelings (both emotional and physical) and behaviours – and instead of leaving them all as a big jumbled mess in your brain, sorting them out and linking them up so that you can see any connections between, say, an event and a thought, or a thought and a behaviour.

This may sound complex, but don't worry. It is actually very easy and once you have done one or two, you will find these maps an easy way of identifying 'problem-maintaining' thoughts and behaviours so that you can start to work on adjusting them. You are going to map out the links between these things. However, the map of your difficulties is not set in concrete and you will constantly change and add to it as you work through the book and become more aware of the contribution to your views and outlook of various life events.

Key idea

Creating a model of your problem that includes all aspects of it gives a great basis for making changes. Creating this model is the basic driving force of the CBT therapy process, and you can learn to use this yourself.

Conceptualizations come in all shapes and sizes so don't worry if the next book you read or course that you go on shows one that is different to look at. They all work on the same principle and achieve the same result – an explanation of what is going on.

Here is a simple model to give you the idea.

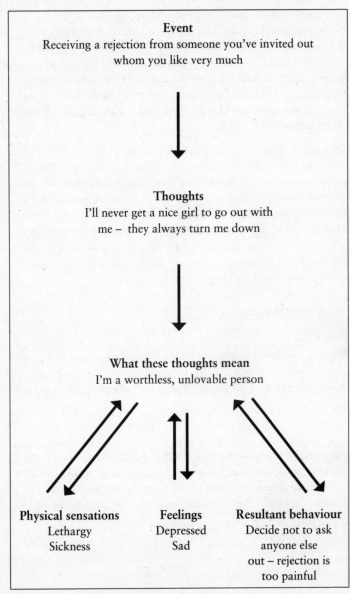

Event
Receiving a rejection from someone you've invited out
whom you like very much

↓

Thoughts
I'll never get a nice girl to go out with
me – they always turn me down

↓

What these thoughts mean
I'm a worthless, unlovable person

Physical sensations
Lethargy
Sickness

Feelings
Depressed
Sad

Resultant behaviour
Decide not to ask
anyone else
out – rejection is
too painful

Example of a conceptualization or map of worries

MAKE YOUR OWN MAP

Create your own conceptualization for a recent negative event, using the headings in the example and filling in the detail. As mentioned previously, you need to be very specific and exact – CBT doesn't like generalizations, as they are fuzzy and hard to work with. So find a specific event and evaluate your thinking in a very specific way; for example, don't write 'I felt wishy washy', write 'I felt sad and humiliated'. Use language that describes exactly what your thoughts and feelings were and don't generalize. The importance of this is that it makes these thoughts and feelings more easily identifiable when it comes to making changes.

A conceptualization is just a map. It shows you where you are, how you have got here, why you have stopped, and what alternative routes onwards there might be. Formulating your problems in this way will enable you to work out far more clearly what is going on, why these things are going on, and what you might begin to do to make changes. It gives you a sense of control because you have narrowed all your difficult thoughts, feelings and actions down to a very specific framework that you can actually look at, on the paper in front of you. So clarity goes up and ideas for change become easier to spot.

Idiosyncratic thinking

We all have our own way of seeing the world, as the following case study shows.

Case study

When Bill met Pete looking glum in the High Street one lunchtime, he gave him his usual 'How are you?'. Pete's response was 'I'm feeling really down – very depressed and anxious'. It turned out that Pete's boss had bawled him out that morning over a poor piece of work and Pete felt this must mean that he was a poor employee, probably going to be put on the redundancy list, wouldn't be able to pay his mortgage, etc. Poor man!

As he walked further, Bill meet David and asked the same 'How are you?' question. David's reply was 'I'm feeling really angry!'. It turned out that David's boss had bawled him out that morning over a poor piece of work and David felt that his boss was being hugely unfair, not taking into account just how difficult the piece had been, how much effort he had put in and how good his work normally was. He was furious with his boss!

Finally, Bill met John. 'How are you, John,' said Bill. 'Just fine,' said John, 'I did have a moment this morning, when my boss really bawled me out for a poor piece of work I had done but he's always very crabby on Monday mornings, plus he did have a point; I didn't do as well as usual, so I'll take it on board and put more effort in next time'.

The case study shows us:

- ▶ three people experiencing exactly the same life event

- ▶ three completely different interpretations of the personal meaning of the event

- ▶ three completely different effects of the event on their emotional well-being.

This is an example of what we call 'idiosyncratic thinking'. Everyone has different ways of interpreting their experiences. Different people give their own interpretation to the same experience. This is why discovering the meaning *to you* of what has happened or might happen is all-important. Unfortunately, we don't always interpret our experiences positively.

Remember, it doesn't matter how much you believe something – you can believe it with all your heart and soul – but that doesn't make it true. It just makes it your own, unique point of view, and this point of view may be neither correct nor helpful.

Take a look at the conceptualization (map) you have made for yourself. Now answer the following questions:

- ▶ Does writing things up in this way give me a clearer idea of the connection between my personal thoughts about something and the way I am feeling?

- ▶ Can I understand how my action(s) was the result of the way I saw things?

- ▶ Does it now make more sense that if my thoughts and feelings were negative and my actions followed suit, I am most likely maintaining my problems or my unhappiness, rather than finding a way out of it?

- ▶ Knowing what I know now, what might I think or do a little differently to give me an outcome that is at least marginally better?

MAKING CONNECTIONS – 'JOINING THE DOTS'

You are now becoming familiar with the idea that CBT practice starts with beginning to observe your responses to disturbing situations and how this draws your attention to the connection between cognitions, moods and behaviours.

Remember this

Because thoughts, feelings and actions are all connected, when we make changes for the better in one area, it will have a positive effect on the other areas.

You will find the easiest way to develop conceptualizations of your problems is by asking yourself questions such as the following.

▶ What is it in my life that is disturbing me?

▶ Going back to my youth or childhood, can I identify any ongoing difficulties, for example, shyness or low self-esteem, that might contribute to my present circumstances?

▶ Could these learned traits hold an explanation of how I think or act in the present?

▶ What are my default emotions? Do I tend to feel depressed or anxious, angry or nervous? Identify your emotions specifically, using just one word for each.

▶ What about my thinking style? How do I generally tend to look at things? Do I usually see the bright side, or the problems ahead?

▶ Do I tend to resolve my worries or do I more often feel that nothing seems to help?

Use your conceptualization diagram to work through a variety of specific situations. You will begin to see a pattern in your responses and to identify certain beliefs (more on those in Chapter 9) that may contribute to the maintenance of your problems.

One of the problems people sometimes have is *not* being able to define exactly why they feel as they do. This, of course, makes it equally hard to express exactly what they *would* like. If, despite your efforts in this chapter, you still feel this way, please don't worry. CBT is very good at digging out what's really going on when we are uncertain, and we will address this as we go along. CBT skills will help you find the answer.

Focus points

* You will now have a much better idea of the relationship between thoughts, feelings, physical sensations and behaviours. You will understand how they feed off each other and can lead to unhappiness being maintained or even exacerbated.

* You should be able to use this information to draw a sketch or diagram of these links, which will help you see more clearly why certain problems don't go away. Looking at things in this way will give you the beginnings of a way forward to change: adjusting your thinking and/or adjusting what you do. There is an old saying that 'The definition of madness is to do the same old things in the same old ways and expect a different result'. This is what your conceptualization will show you – the same old thinking and the same old actions will give you the same old outcomes.

* You can use what you have learned about goals in Chapter 2 to help yourself set new targets and to give some thought about how these might be achieved.

* The personal meaning of thoughts should now be clear and significant. It is how you *view* something – and that is not necessarily the truth of the situation. This doesn't mean that your viewpoints don't have merit and intellect to support them. It just means that they are not actual facts and so are worthy of re-evaluation, if such re-evaluation may result in you feeling better and more optimistic.

Rate your effort (1–10) for the exercises you have tried in this chapter ......

Next step

One criticism of CBT is levelled by people who tell me that they've worked on trying to adjust their thoughts with good intent and endeavour, but with little effect. The outcome isn't solid enough or positive enough for the effort.

This isn't the fault of CBT but usually occurs because individuals are working with the wrong thoughts and not making careful and balanced re-evaluations. If you feel you are dull and boring, telling yourself one million times that you are witty and interesting won't make you believe it one jot more. If you tell yourself that you are upset because your friend was late for lunch, you will stay upset. To make CBT work for you, you need to get to the deeper meanings of your upsets, i.e. 'I am upset not because my friend was late for lunch but because I perceive this as meaning she doesn't really care about me. If my friend doesn't care about me, this means I am not an especially likeable person'. Now you have a better thought to work with and in Chapter 4 you will learn more about ensuring that you are not wasting your energies by going off in the wrong direction.

Linking thoughts
to emotions

By the end of this chapter you should be able to:

▶ *match thoughts and emotions*
▶ *identify correctly which of your many thoughts is causing you to feel a certain way*

? Self-assessment

1 Do you tend to say 'I see...' or 'I feel...' or 'I think...'?

2 If someone asked you how you felt, would you be more likely to answer them by describing your emotions ('I feel dreadful') or your thoughts ('I've had a really bad day today')?

3 Which would upset you more – missing your holiday flight by (a) 20 minutes, or (b) two minutes?

4 If you are struggling with something, e.g. a work problem, does your mind run immediately to the worst-case scenario ('I may lose my job over this') or do you remain in a swirl of negative emotion such as extreme anxiety?

5 If you had the choice, would you prefer to change the circumstances that worry you or would you prefer to be able to worry less about the circumstances?

The questions above all relate to the idea that we have two minds – a rational mind and an emotional mind. When you have answered these questions, you will have a good idea of whether your responses come from your rational or your emotional mind. For example, if your answer to question 3 was (b), you are someone whose emotional mind tends to run things; if your response was that it wouldn't make any difference to you, then your rational mind tends to be the boss.

Another way of describing this would be to say that there are 'thinkers' and 'feelers'. Knowing which of these you are will help you in this chapter, which focuses on identifying thoughts and feelings, and the links between the two. If you are a 'thinker', you will identify thoughts more easily than emotions. A 'feeler' will do the opposite. So as you work through the exercises, start with the approach you are more comfortable with. There is no 'better' way to be – they are just our habitual ways – but some of us find it easier to identify with our thoughts and then search for the accompanying emotions, while others find it easier to connect with how they feel and then search for what they might have been thinking to engender the feelings.

The power of our thoughts

In Chapter 3 you learned about the power thoughts have in shaping our views and behaviours, and how they can often keep a problem going rather than resolve it. What you have also learned is that by conceptualizing the problem – looking at it and the outcomes it produces in a variety of ways – you can see more clearly the whole picture and make adjustments to any part of it, noting that these adjustments will positively affect other parts of it. You can start anywhere you like. However, it is most usual to start by looking at negative thoughts and making changes there. So first you need to learn how to identify, very specifically, what you are thinking that causes you emotional distress.

You are now familiar with the idea that your thoughts have a great bearing on your emotions. This can also be true in reverse – how you are feeling can decide what you think. When you feel emotionally negative it is likely that both your thoughts and physiology will reflect this. This fact can help you identify your negative thinking. Identify your mood first and then consider what is going on in your life and your mind to make you feel this way.

THOUGHT RECORDS

Writing things down in a structured way is a great tool for recording and working through all sorts of things. In Chapter 3, you made a start on recording thoughts and feelings. An extension of this is filling in a Thought Record. This will help you identify your thoughts through recognizing your moods. However, as it is often easier to focus on mood when emotions are strong, initially I have asked you to identify your moods, rather than your thoughts.

Look at the 'Mood First' Thought Record table below and read the information about filling it in that follows.

Feelings: write down your mood in the first column – more than one description is also fine.

Remember, how you feel also creates physical responses, so check first with any bodily changes – are you feeling tired and lethargic (when it is likely that your mood will be low)? Is your stomach churning and your heart racing (when it is likely that your mood will be anxious)? Questions like these will help you identify your mood.

Situation: write down what is happening, or has just happened, to make you feel this way.

Automatic thoughts: write down what is going through your mind, or what was going through your mind, just before you started to feel this way.

It may help you to work out your thoughts if you ask yourself the following questions:

▶ What was I afraid might be going to happen?

▶ What was happening, or in my mind, just before I began to feel this way?

▶ Am I linking this episode to any past incidents when things turned out badly?

The 'Situation' column in a Thought Record is very important. It helps you to notice patterns of events that trigger certain thoughts and emotions more readily. Is it a specific place, a specific person or a specific location that causes these feelings? If so, you can begin to think constructively about making changes to these circumstances or eliminating them altogether if you can. Even if this isn't possible, you will at least have forewarning of possible thought and mood changes and you may be able to develop an action plan to defeat them.

Try it now

Let's invent an example. Perhaps you received a compliment from your boss about some work you had done. How would you feel when you received the compliment? Perhaps you might feel *hopeful* (at your work being appreciated) or *overwhelmed* (by pressure to perform well). Using this example, identify one or two emotions and think about what kind of thoughts you might have that relate to the mood. If, for example, you felt *hopeful*, you might be thinking:

* This might put me in line for a salary increase.
* Hopefully, I will now be considered for the promotion I want.
* It's very nice to be appreciated.

If you felt *overwhelmed*, your thoughts could be:

* I was just lucky – I'll probably fail next time.
* I hate people having expectations of me.
* I will have to work much harder now to keep this standard up.

Look at the Thought Record below to see how this can all be recorded so that the situation–thoughts–feelings triad comes in to play. I have used the example given in the box above to start you off.

Feelings	Situation	Automatic thoughts
Write one word, e.g. happy, sad, anxious, overjoyed	This may be an actual event, or just an image in your mind	What was going through your mind just before you started to feel this way?
Delighted	Boss has praised my work	Perhaps I will get a promotion or a raise
or	or	or
Fearful	Boss has praised my work	I will be under great pressure now to keep to this standard of work and I don't think I am up to it

A 'Mood First' Thought Record

Try it now

Now create your own 'Mood First' Thought Record.

Look back at a recent event that caused you to feel some emotion (it doesn't have to be negative one).

Draw up a similar table in your workbook and fill in from your own example the thoughts and feelings arising from the situation.

If you wrote down more than one thought or feeling, draw a circle round the strongest one. The purpose of this is to ensure that:

▶ you focus on the thoughts and feelings that cause you the most upset

▶ your thoughts and feelings match.

Rating your thoughts and feelings

We have seen already the importance of identifying the 'strong' thought – the one that holds the most meaning and accountability for your emotions. One way of doing this is by rating the strength of your thoughts and emotions on a scale of 0 per cent to 100 per cent. If you note that you feel anxious (20 per cent) and angry (80 per cent), then your anger is the 'strong' emotion and the one you should be paying attention to.

There are many good reasons for doing this; for example, to enable you to make comparisons between different thoughts and feelings, or 'before and after' ratings when you have made thinking and/or behavioural changes.

You can be this exact when you become more confident in the rating process. But for the moment, just be aware of the thought or feeling that stands out as stronger than the others and put a circle round it or them.

plane' would be a 'stronger' thought and a better match for the anxiety. Many people waste weeks and months filling in Thought Records that are of no help to them because they are not identifying the thought that is the critical one in engendering the emotion.

The causal thought

Another way of describing what we identify as the 'strong' thought is as a *causal* thought. It is, in effect, the base thought that *causes* the emotions, the physiology and probably the actions that follow. It is the significant thought, and ensuring that we have identified it correctly is vital to overcoming the negativity it engenders.

Try it now

'Matching' thoughts and moods is very important. Try to identify the causal thought in the following examples. For each emotion, pick the thought that you think most closely matches the severity rating of the emotion.

Emotion Anxiety (80%)

Thought 1 'I don't know if I'm good enough to get the promotion I'm hoping for.'

Thought 2 'Not getting the promotion I want will be a personal disaster.'

Emotion Depression (75%)

Thought 1 'I really don't think this essay is going to get me the A grade I need.'

Thought 2 'If I don't get an A grade for this essay I'm afraid I will fail the course.'

Emotion Embarrassment (100%)

Thought 1 'I couldn't think of anything sensible to say to that girl I wanted to impress.'

Thought 2 'I can't get over having made such a complete fool of myself.'

Emotion Fear (80%)

Thought 1 'I'm always nervous when travelling by train.'

Thought 2 'I can't stop thinking that the train might crash.'

I suspect that, had there not been a second thought option for each emotion, you would have been happy to agree that the first thought was a good match. However, now look at all those first thoughts again.

There is nothing in them that suggests that their owner might be severely depressed, highly anxious, totally embarrassed or full of fear. They are simply comments.

In each case, it is the second thought that creates the high emotion – and is thus the correct thought to capture and work on.

THE DOWNWARD ARROW TECHNIQUE

The Downward Arrow technique is another, well-known technique (which some of you may already know or use) for identifying the strongest thought, the thought that creates the high emotion. It is a very useful tool, so keep it in your metaphorical 'toolbox' and bring it out when you need it.

Here is an example:

> You are feeling stressed, anxious and your head is aching.
>
> Your thought is: 'I am never going to get all this work done in the timescale I've been given.'

Doesn't that sound about right? You are feeling exceedingly stressed (say 80 per cent) and the reason for that is that you have too much work to do and too little time to do it in. That makes sense. But (using the exercise you completed above) you now know that this isn't necessarily the case. Thinking that you won't have enough time to get some work done might concern you, but it might not. In itself it may not be a problem.

▶ 'I'll simply have to say I cannot do it.'

▶ 'I'll just have to carry on tomorrow and rearrange my schedule to encompass it.'

To work out why this situation is the cause of such highly rated emotion, you ask yourself some further questions.

Your downward arrow
Following your initial thought...

↓

The next question is: *'Why does this matter?'*

↓

The answer may be: *'If I don't get this information
put together in time for the client meeting,
they won't have the correct figures to work with.'*

↓

Now ask yourself a further question: *'Why does that matter?'*

↓

The answer may be: *'Without this detailed information,
our clients won't appreciate how
successful we've been on their behalf.'*

↓

Don't stop – ask a third question: *'Why does that matter?'*

↓

The answer may be: *'The client may switch agencies and
that could leave me without a job.'*

Now you have a strong thought. You have finally reached a level of thought which makes complete sense in the context of feeling such a high degree of emotion. It would, of course, be serious if the client didn't have the full information he was entitled to expect, but the possibility of losing one's job over it would be even more serious.

To enable you to work on challenging and modifying these thoughts, this first step is crucial: *find the strong thought* – the thought that causes you to feel such high emotion. In this case, it has little to do with the shortage of time to complete the job and everything to do with your view of the very negative outcome that might result.

Hopefully, you can now understand:

- how helpful it is to identify our strong thoughts and moods
- how the strength of a mood can be an excellent indicator of the strength of the thought we should be trying to identify.

Try it now

Some of us tend to think in pictures rather than words. If this is you, then you can use imagery to recall a situation in your mind. Close your eyes and picture yourself in the situation and bring back into your mind the events around you and the emotions you felt. Relive the situation as closely as you can. Bring back into your mind the aspects of where you were – the layout of the room, office or garden, for example. Who else was there? By reliving the experience almost like a movie in your head, you may find it easier to identify the thoughts and emotions that were going through your mind.

Focus points

- We have taken time in this chapter to familiarize you with being able to identify the all-important 'strong' thought. This is because **unless you can do this** (notice the bold type!) you could be working with the wrong thought(s) and will achieve little. Make sure you have the right thought before you go any further.

* You have also learned to match your thoughts to your emotions (and vice versa). Again, this is an essential thing for you to be able to do. You may miss the strong thought if you don't rate correctly the emotion that results from it.
* You are beginning to practise regularly so that identifying your thoughts comes more easily to you.
* Where you have difficulty working out precisely what you were thinking, using imagery may be helpful.
* Learn to rate your thoughts and moods so that you can identify easily whether you have a good match or need to look further – perhaps using the Downward Arrow technique to assist you.

Rate your effort (1–10) for the exercises you have tried in this chapter ......

Next step

You will now be completely familiar with identifying causal thoughts and their linked emotions, and also with working out what caused them in the first place. Now that you have mastered these abilities, your next task is to learn what to do with what you can now discover; how to 'turn things around' so that negative thoughts learn their rightful place in your mind, which is way down the pecking order. You will learn to say 'Really?' when negative thoughts tempt you to see them as facts. You will learn how to re-evaluate thoughts and how to see things in a much more optimistic way, even when negative thoughts may have their own validity.

Dealing with negative thoughts

By the end of this chapter you should be able to:

▶ *challenge the validity of negative automatic thoughts (NATs)*

▶ *talk back to NATs*

Self-assessment

1 In the past, have you accepted your thinking as valid even when it has made you anxious or depressed?

2 Does the idea of questioning negative thoughts and looking for alternatives sound a difficult concept?

3 Does the rationale behind challenging negative thoughts make sense to you?

4 Are you hoping that CBT will help you to prove how wrong your negative thoughts are?

5 Are you willing to work hard at this chapter?

If the answer to question 1 is 'yes', you are perfectly normal and an ideal person to be reading this book. Don't worry if the answer to question 2 is 'yes'; if it was 'no', you would be less likely to be reading this book! If the answer to 3 is 'no', you need to go back a little and make sure you understand how negative thoughts account for your negative emotions. If you answered 'yes' to question 4, that is fine – but wrong!; you will find the more balanced answer as you read through this chapter. Question 5 is almost rhetorical as I would be disappointed if you answered 'no', but it should not put you off in any way; there is nothing too difficult or too time-consuming in this chapter. The key things here are consistency and regularity; little and often will enable you to see a real improvement quite quickly.

Negative thoughts – are they really true?

By now you should have a good understanding of:

▶ the different types of thoughts we have

▶ how powerful negative thoughts can be in getting us to believe them

▶ how such thoughts can affect our emotions in a dramatic, negative way and make us feel highly anxious or depressed

▶ the importance of the fact that they are simply thoughts, and not necessarily facts or truths.

In Chapter 4 you also learned how to identify the most powerful negative thought in your mind at any time – the one that caused you to feel highly emotional. You learned the importance of identifying this 'strong' thought. Believing pessimistic thinking without testing it against reality will send you down the wrong track and may wrongly cause you long periods of stress and upset. So the skill of thought-challenging is a vital part of being able to think in a more balanced and optimistic way.

We are not certain why people think in such different ways – some naturally optimistic, others cautious or balanced, and some generally negative. It may be due to our biological or genetic inheritance, but also, and most often, to our environment: our upbringing, early adulthood and specific, meaningful events. All of these come together to develop our thinking style. What we do know is that these thinking styles can become habits. But with a certain amount of work and effort, bad habits can be broken and negative thinking styles can be changed.

We all look at the world in a different way because we give our own interpretation to our experiences. People can respond quite differently to exactly the same situation because they are using their own life view rather than a more general one. Where these personal views form a pattern of negativity, CBT helps us to identify unhelpful thought patterns and beliefs, and to find alternative ways of thinking and perceiving that work for us.

So how do we start achieving this?

Try it now

Next time you find yourself becoming tense, worried or depressed, sit down as soon as you can and fill in your Thought Record. Describe the physical sensations you experienced and the thoughts which went through your head at the time.

Don't worry if you find this difficult at first. It may be quite a new idea to try to recall what you were thinking when you were worried or feeling low, and it may take some practice before you get the hang of it.

Here is a Thought Record you can use to practise 'thought-challenging'. It is different from the Thought Records you have used so far as they vary depending on what we want to look at. We call this a classic, basic, five-column Thought Record and it is a good one to start off your work.

This Thought Record is to help you begin to find alternative ways of looking at your problems. Look at the model below and then draw up your own Thought Record in your workbook that you can tailor to yourself. Don't forget to circle the strongest thought and/or emotion (or give them percentage ratings) as a clear indicator of the most upsetting.

Event	Negative thought(s)	Negative feeling(s)	Is there any other way that I can look at this?	How do I feel now?
Example: My partner forgets our anniversary	He's so useless	Anger Frustration	Actually, there are other things he is good at.	Calmer, more forgiving
	He obviously doesn't love me	Sadness Worthlessness	He often tells me that he loves me, he's just rather forgetful	More confident: I realize that I read too much into things

60

Action plan: Is there anything you could now do differently to make a difference? Write down any ideas that you have in your workbook.

Hopefully this makes sense to you and you won't find it too difficult. You need to practise this a great deal before it becomes second nature.

Remember this

You aren't trying to eliminate your negative thinking, you are simply checking to see if there is a more balanced, more likely alternative. When our mood is low, or we habitually think in a certain way, we are very good at discounting positives and noticing only the negatives. This practice will help to re-balance your brain so that it is more even-handed in its considerations. Gradually, as your brain gets used to doing this, it will become more of a default way of thinking and the pessimistic thoughts will take a back seat.

WORK, WORK, WORK!

At this point we are asking you to start undertaking some serious, life-changing work. This is more than simply understanding a principle, as you have done up to now. This is about acting on your understanding, and the more work you put in the quicker things will change.

My own clients often ask me questions about this that are important. So here are some of the questions they ask me, and the answers, which I hope you will find encouraging.

▶ **Finding time to write things down isn't easy; how long will this go on?**

Bear in mind that you are retraining your brain to think differently. To start with it is going to fight you! Your brain has held on to its pessimistic, unhelpful thoughts and beliefs for a long time. However, you will gradually find thought-challenging increasingly easy, until you realize that you can do it in your head automatically. At this point you can dispense with writing things down on a regular basis, unless your brain gets lazy and starts returning to its old ways, when you can reintroduce this technique.

There is a well-known learning model called the *Four Stages of Learning*. Understanding these stages may be helpful to you in evaluating your progress (and not giving up too soon). These stages are:

1 **Being unconsciously incompetent.** This means using skewed, pessimistic thinking styles without even being aware that this is why you feel so badly.

2 **Becoming consciously incompetent.** This is the point at which you start to realize that you may be making thinking and behavioural errors, but you aren't in possession of any skills or information to enable you to change things.

3 **Becoming consciously competent.** Once you become consciously competent you are doing well. This is the point at which you are mastering much more positive ways of feeling and behaving, but the downside is that this only happens when you *consciously* focus on what you are doing or thinking. When you forget, you go back to the bad old ways. For this reason, this stage of learning is the hardest – and some people do give up here. They find the change too challenging and decide to embrace their weaknesses and live with them as that appears to be an easier alternative. So don't give up! If you persevere, you will eventually come to the final stage of learning.

4 **Becoming unconsciously competent.** At last it is no longer hard work: no more writing things down, no more slippage when you are not concentrating. Your brain now has a new default setting and it reacts in new, helpful ways without being prodded or coaxed to do so. Wonderful!

▶ **Do I need to carry my Thought Record with me all the time and fill it in immediately?**

No, you don't need to do this. It is better for you to make a mental note of your negative thoughts and actions at the time that they happen, but to work on the 'How else could I look at this?' aspect of the Thought Record when you have some quiet time to yourself so that you don't rush your responses and can give real thought to it all. On the other hand, don't leave it too long or your memories will fade. Find a quiet time each day if you can.

Many people find it easiest to have a notebook at their bedside and make their notes at the end of the day. Having a regular, usually peaceful time to do this will help greatly. So do it when you can. As with all other tasks, the more you do it, the quicker the changes will come. But don't let it dominate your life. The best idea is to try to take a look at your Thought Record each evening and recall any instances in the day that you might like to record. You will still have a good enough memory of how you felt and what was going through your mind.

▶ **I haven't had any traumas recently. Shall I just wait until something comes up?**

Never wait for a crisis! Firstly, you are right, crises don't (hopefully) come along very often so you won't get much chance to practise re-evaluating your thinking if you wait for one. Instead, search for the smallest thing. If you have a pessimistic or anxiety-driven way of thinking, it will be with you most of the time. You simply get so used to thinking this way that you don't realize that your thoughts aren't rational and valid. Finding yourself feeling depressed because you forgot to drink your coffee and now it is cold is just as valid a thought to note and evaluate as the feelings that accompany redundancy worries or a relationship breaking up. You might just be sitting at home with a drink when negative thoughts come into your mind. Write them down. The thought itself doesn't have to be momentous.

Key idea

The more you use your Thought Record, the more quickly your brain will catch on to this new way of looking at things – large or small.

▶ **Tell me more about this new, fourth column on the Thought Record?**

The Thought Record in Chapter 5 gives you the opportunity not only to record your negative thoughts and emotions but also to examine how realistic they are. Are they facts or simply a first point of view? If the latter, there may be other points of view, other ways of looking at this same situation. We call this a balanced response – a reply that you can make to these thoughts which is usually based on firm evidence.

▶ **I understand the principle but it is often hard to come up with alternatives.**

This is very common, so don't worry. It happens because your own style of thinking has been your habit for so long that it is easy to fall into a negative viewpoint and very hard to see that there could be any alternative. However, you can prompt yourself by asking questions that may elicit answers to help you. Here are some examples.

▶ Is my first thought a fact or an assumption?

▶ If it's just an assumption, might there be an alternative assumption?

▶ Have I had a similar experience before when I have taken a different view?

▶ If so, how did I see things then, and why?

▶ Is there anything positive about this situation that I may be discounting or ignoring?

▶ Am I prone to jumping to conclusions rather than considering alternatives?

▶ If a friend told me that she had my worries and concerns, what would I say to her?

▶ If I confided my worries to my friend, what would she be likely to say to me?

▶ If I asked a few of my friends if they felt the way I do about what had happened, would they all agree with me or might there be a diversity of opinion? Why?

▶ What is the worst thing that could happen if my negative thoughts are correct?

▶ Could I cope with it? Would it really change my life?

▶ Will I still care about it in a few years time?

▶ Am I really 100 per cent certain that...?

Try it now

Take one instance of recent negative thinking and write down in your workbook an answer to each of the questions above.

You should now have a better idea of how answering your negative thoughts in a more helpful, realistic way can help you to cope with your worries.

▶ **But my negative thoughts are true; I am not looking at this pessimistically.**

You may be quite right. This may occasionally (or often) be the case. Sometimes, it can be very hard to find balanced alternatives to the negative thoughts we have because we actually *are* in a jam or a tight spot. The purpose of CBT is not just to identify and dismantle negative thoughts as wrong or skewed and then to come up with a positive alternative that will make you feel better. That would be a poor return for your hard work. In essence, the role of CBT is to ensure that we evaluate our thinking critically in the most open-minded way. It encourages us to look for all possible alternatives and to develop a balanced viewpoint; that might lead us to conclude that, indeed, things are pretty bad. In such a case, CBT will work with you to find a solution to your difficulty, to the tight spot you are in, that might involve behavioural changes or developing resilience – the ability to cope with difficulties rather than sinking under their weight. So don't worry. CBT won't let you down.

When you have to accept that your original thoughts were an accurate reflection of the situation, you can develop an action plan. You will see that at the bottom of the Thought Record there is a question to prompt ideas for an action plan. Ask yourself what you might be able to do to mitigate against what has happened and develop some options for putting it right.

Sometimes your action plan can be little more than acceptance. I'm a great believer in the idea of 'acceptance and resilience'. Acceptance is a quality of strength, not weakness. It can take courage to accept a difficult situation with equanimity. Resilience then comes into play – the quality you need to help you stand your ground in the face of adversity and not to let things beat you.

One way to achieve this is with coping statements. Here are some examples of coping statements which enable you to deal with your worries in a more positive and constructive way.

▶ I'm going to face this problem situation and deal with it as best as I can.

▶ It may not work completely, but I shall do my best and see what happens.

▶ Worry makes me feel worse so I will accept the situation rather than fret about it.

▶ I've been in a position like this before and have come out of it in one piece.

▶ Things will improve the more I get used to coping with my difficulties.

▶ As I develop my confidence and resilience I'll feel proud of myself.

▶ Most things don't turn out nearly as badly as we think they will.

▶ I'm strong enough to cope no matter what.

Key idea

Being able to think in a more balanced way requires practice. As well as using your Thought Record, get used to the idea of stopping to challenge your thinking on a regular basis when you recognize (as you will more easily now) negative or anxious thinking. Also, before going into a situation that makes you anxious or worried, think beforehand about how you will answer any negative thoughts before, during and afterwards.

▶ **I try to come up with more balanced alternative viewpoints but I still don't feel better.**

Don't worry; this is a very common difficulty. If you don't really believe what you are writing even though it all sounds very balanced and evaluative, it is because your NATs are very firmly entrenched in your mind and are able to override your new thought suggestions. In Chapter 9 we look at the beliefs and assumptions that drive our thinking, which are far more absolute and intransigent ideas, and you will find that you can use some belief-shifting skills to help you with your NATs as well.

For the moment, make your alternative thoughts something that you will have some genuine belief in. If your negative thought is 'Nobody likes me', you are more likely to believe an alternative thought along the lines of 'I'm sure some people like me at least some of the time' than an extreme alternative such as 'Of course everybody likes me'. Be thoughtful when considering alternatives. Ask yourself 'Could I have at least some faith in this idea?'.

Don't worry too much at this stage. As you work through the book you will come across a variety of other, quite compelling techniques for getting our brains to become more open-minded in believing alternatives. You are just starting out as yet and even the smallest, most occasional success at the moment is a real advancement.

Try it now

1 Practise filling in Thought Records as often as you can. However, don't do it just because it has been suggested here. Spend a little quiet time first going over in your mind why and how you think this might help you. Review your ability to recognize the most troublesome thought, and go back over this again if you become unsure. Never do anything without understanding its benefits. In this regard also, less is more. Better a few entries that you have really thought about and that really make a difference, than writing masses and losing your way in the middle of it all.

2 Look again at the Four Stages of Learning. Stage 3 is the one that most people find the hardest, as they are now beginning to expect things to go right but often that isn't the case. The balance between what you put in and what you get back can often seem lopsided at this stage. It is at this point that many people give up, preferring to live with their worries and limitations rather than to persevere to overcome them. In these instances, it might help you to recall other competencies that you are now very adept at and take for granted, yet which at one point in your life had to be painstakingly learned. My own example would be learning to drive. Trying to do several things at once without the car stalling seemed to me, as a young woman, almost impossible. All that kept me going was my thinking: 'Everyone else is out on the roads driving so eventually this *must* become quite simple.' And it did. Do any of us even think about our actions and reactions as we drive along now? Encourage yourself with examples such as these that are personal to you, and they will keep you going.

Remember this

If there is anything still puzzling you, read over again what you have learned, and ensure that you understand it fully before you spend time on the written exercises.

Recognizing faulty thinking styles

While we tend to believe that our thoughts are unbiased, this is often not true. Even when we recognize our thinking as negative, we still assume that it is rational and correct. Psychologists have discovered that most of us suffer at least some of the time from 'cognitive bias', which is another way of saying that our thoughts are not necessarily correct and may be heavily skewed for a variety of reasons. Depending on our self-worth, we can be very self-deprecating or, where we have anger or irritability problems, we can become easily frustrated by others. Learn to recognize these faulty thinking styles and then be honest with yourself about which apply to you. The faulty thinking styles described below may be familiar as they are similar to others that are commonly found in books and articles on this subject. When I first came across a list of these thinking styles and applied it to myself, I found that I could tick almost everything on it! Instead of making me feel embarrassed, it made me smile. I realized how many of us have the same biased thinking about a great many things.

The descriptions will show you how your NATs can fall into a pattern of thinking styles which, although they distort reality, are very easy to believe.

A further problem is that once we start making thinking errors, we tend to stick with them. They become assumptions and beliefs that we retain unless we make an effort to recognize them and change them.

GENERALIZING THE SPECIFIC

You generalize the specific when you come to a general conclusion based on a single incident or piece of evidence. You use words such as 'always' and 'never', 'nobody' and 'everyone' to make an all-embracing rule out of a specific situation. If you make a mistake, you tell yourself that you are hopeless. If you get rejected, you tell yourself that you are unlovable.

Examples

▶ You fall off your bike while going round a sharp corner and decide you are an incompetent cyclist and won't cycle again.

▶ You notice a small dirty mark on the kitchen surface and consider yourself slovenly.

▶ Someone is rude to you and you consider yourself unlikeable.

MIND-READING

This is one of the commonest thinking errors we make when our self-esteem is low. Without their saying so, we 'know' what people are thinking and why they act the way they do. In particular, we are able to divine how people are feeling towards us. It is fatal to self-esteem because we believe that others agree with our negative opinions of ourselves.

Yet we are jumping to conclusions without any real evidence. And, for some reason, we only seem to have the gift of mind-reading *negative* views. Interestingly, we never seem to develop a talent for mind-reading *positive* thoughts!

Examples

▶ 'I know he thinks I'm not up to the job.'

▶ 'I can tell she thinks I am unattractive.'

▶ 'I'm sure they feel that they are stuck with me.'

MAGNIFICATION AND FILTERING

We take the negative details from a situation and magnify them, while at the same time filtering out all the positive aspects. We focus on the one thing that went badly in an otherwise successful presentation. We dismiss all our achievements and focus bleakly on the one thing that we are not particularly good at.

Example

▶ You've just come back from the hairdressers and feel fresh and attractive. You are looking forward to going out with your friends and feel sure that they will all think how nice you look. However, when you get in your partner makes no comment about your new hairstyle. Your negative thoughts immediately latch on to the fact that you must look unattractive and he is too polite to say so – or he would have said *something* surely? This means you must look a fright and the thought of even bothering to go out now seems a waste of time if you will just be seen as ugly and unattractive.

POLARIZED THINKING

Sometimes called 'all or nothing thinking', it is when we think of people, situations or events in extremes of good or bad: 'I must be perfect or I am a failure', 'If I'm not beautiful, I'm ugly'. There is no middle ground. The problem is that we usually find ourselves at the negative end of our polarized extremes. So if you cannot be all good, you must be all bad.

Examples

▶ If you don't win the club tennis tournament you might as well give up the game.

▶ If your relationship doesn't work out, you will never find true love.

CATASTROPHIZING

We expect disaster. We believe that things will almost certainly go wrong if they possibly can, and that if they do we will not be able to cope. So not only do we over-estimate the likelihood of calamity, we multiply it by our perceived idea of the catastrophic consequences. Whenever we notice or hear about a problem, we start thinking 'what if' and then decide that if this terrible thing did happen to us, we would not be able to cope.

Examples

▶ 'What if I were to get seriously sick? I couldn't bear it and would be better off dead.'

▶ 'What if everything goes wrong? I know I won't be able to deal with disaster.'

PERSONALIZATION

This involves thinking that everything people do or say is some kind of reaction to us.

Examples

▶ Your husband refers to a new girl in the office with short dark hair. As yours is long and blonde, you immediately assume that he doesn't like your hairstyle.

▶ Someone tells you that your boss isn't happy with the monthly sales figures and you instantly feel that what he's really unhappy with is your own poor performance.

BLAMING

This is the opposite of personalization. We hold other people, organizations – or even the universe – responsible for our problems. We feel unable to change our views or our circumstances, as we see ourselves as victims of other people's thoughtlessness and meanness.

Examples

▶ 'She has made me feel terrible.'

▶ 'That company ruined my life.'

▶ 'If he hadn't done what he did, I wouldn't have reacted that way.'

SELF-BLAME
In this case, instead of feeling a victim, you feel responsible for the pain and happiness of everyone around you.

Examples

▶ If your son fails a school exam you feel to blame for not making him study more.

▶ If a friend is disappointed at the low turnout for their birthday party, you feel that you should have personally ensured more people were invited.

RIGID THINKING
We feel resentful because we think we know what's right but other people won't agree with us. We continually attempt to prove that our opinions and actions are correct. We expect other people to change their views and actions if we pressurize or cajole them enough. We try to change people in this way when we believe our hopes for happiness depend entirely on their behaving differently.

Examples

▶ 'I can't understand why people don't see things my way. There must be something wrong with me.'

▶ 'I can't understand why people don't see things my way. There must be something wrong with them.'

A positive way forward

While it can be hard to discover that much of your thinking is biased by negative distortions, acknowledging this is the first step to change. The next step is to use this knowledge to help you tackle your thoughts.

How do you do this? By working to familiarize yourself with these cognitive distortions. Once you understand them and can recall them easily, you will begin to spot them when they crop up. They are easier for you to identify than some of your NATs because of the patterns they follow, and you can take an 'oh, I recognize what I'm doing!' attitude to them and then rethink what has actually happened.

Most people, when presented with these styles of faulty thinking and asked to acknowledge any that apply to them, find themselves smiling as they recognize these common thinking errors that most of us make a lot of the time. They are normal! We all do it. Now you can become more aware of them and knock them on the head quite easily.

Try it now

From now on, each time you fill in a Thought Record, put a small note beside the thought(s) that indicates which particular style of faulty thinking it is. For example:

Negative Thought	Cognitive Bias
'I cannot cook at all.'	Generalizing the specific
'My lamb stew was so dry.'	Polarized thinking
'I know they all thought I didn't know what I was talking about.'	Mind reading
'I wouldn't have acted that way if Jenny had been a bit nicer to me.'	Blaming

Focus points

* You have learned more about the idea that no matter how 'true' your negative thoughts seem to you, they may not be. Remember, you can believe something with your heart and soul but that doesn't make it a fact, simply your own view.

* Thought-challenging can be hard but don't give up. Make a crib-sheet of questions such as the ones suggested in this chapter, and keep chipping away at those negative thoughts.

* Re-evaluating your thinking isn't the sum total of the skills you will develop with CBT but it is a powerful start, a cornerstone of new thinking, and it will help you to evaluate situations far more intelligently.

* The more you practise, the more quickly things will start to change for you.

* Do appreciate that using a Thought Record is just a preliminary to beginning to think in a more open way as your default. Once this becomes easier, it also becomes important to start practising without writing things down. Once you have achieved this you will have made a huge stride forward.

* Many of your negative thoughts will fall into one of the faulty thinking categories we have referred to in this chapter. This will make it easier for you to recognize where you are going wrong with your thinking, and to put it right.

* The very familiarity of these thinking errors may be quite comforting to you. Most of us make them at some point, many of us quite often. Becoming more aware of them in day-to-day life will give you confidence that you can spot them, challenge them and re-evaluate them without much difficulty.

Rate your effort (1–10) for the exercises you have tried in this chapter ......

Next step

In Chapter 6 you turn detective! You will learn how to evaluate the real facts behind the negative thoughts and assumptions that cloud them. In essence, you will be able to start saying to yourself 'If this is so and that is so, then how can such and such be as it is?'. This is where things become very interesting!

Strengthening your balanced thinking

By the end of this chapter you should be far more open to 'playing detective' and looking for evidence that your negative thinking is (or is not) true.

When we are thinking in a well-balanced, rational way, it doesn't matter too much what our initial beliefs are as we will tend to evaluate them and be prepared to change. But when our mood is low and our thoughts are negative, a lack of mental questioning ability and having a closed mind will convince us that the negative information we receive, either from ourselves or from others, is true. So if you answered 'yes' to questions 1–3 and rated yourself below 6 for questions 4 and 5, this chapter is a useful one for you. It will teach you the vital skill of searching for evidence to strengthen your new, more optimistic thinking and weaken your old, pessimistic thinking.

Checking for evidence

Many people start out encouragingly with their Thought Records, believing that these will turn their thinking around quickly and easily. However, no matter how diligently they work on challenging their negative thoughts, after a while they find themselves thinking something along the lines of 'I may have come up with several alternatives to my negative automatic thoughts – but this is just a paper exercise. I don't really *believe* these alternative options'.

It is widely accepted that when you're working on making a shift from negative to positive thinking, especially if your negative views are deep-seated, there is one question that is particularly helpful in re-balancing your whole thinking, and that is: **Where's the evidence?**

Imagine that you are a detective. No matter how certain you are that Joe Burglar did the robbery, you need evidence to prove it. Sometimes a detective can have a strong belief about something that conflicting evidence subsequently proves to be completely wrong. The detective will then go with the evidence.

Imagine being before a judge in a court of law. When the judge asks you what evidence you have to support your case, then saying, 'I simply believe it very strongly' or 'Well, that did happen to me once before' isn't going to result in anything other than 'case dismissed'. Why? No actual evidence.

Remember this

Facts are facts. Anything else is simply a point of view – which might be based on unreliable evidence or on no evidence at all. There is no arguing with facts.

Case study

David was worried about his wife, Jane. She had seemed very pre-occupied lately and was often out. One of their mutual friends, Brian, had been ringing up a lot and Jane seemed to find quite flimsy excuses to go round to his house. The more David thought about it, the clearer the answer became: Jane must be having an affair with Brian. David felt sick with worry. He also felt pretty worthless, as Jane wasn't making much of an effort to hide it from him – all her 'I'm just popping out' messages – and if David suggested coming along too, he was firmly rebuffed. So there it was then. David, soon to be 50 years old, was going to find himself left for another man.

David did try to find other reasons for Jane's constant requirement to spend time with Brian, but nothing he could think of seemed to stack up. All the evidence pointed to this worst-case scenario.

David finally decided that he must confront Jane. He found a quiet time, laid out all the 'evidence' before her and asked her if she was looking for a divorce. Jane at first appeared bemused and then she started to laugh.

She gave David a big hug and told him he was an idiot, but apologized for the confusion; Jane and Brian had been planning an extra special 50th birthday celebration for David and had been quietly collaborating to ensure that the event was booked properly and that all his family and closest friends would be there.

Let's look at David's 'evidence'. While he felt that it was strong, there were no facts to prove the affair, only assumptions made by David that were fuelled by poor self-esteem and a wrongful belief that his wife might be capable of such a thing. In reality, David had no factual evidence at all. Once an alternative explanation presented itself, the evidence here was overwhelming in that it was based on facts – restaurant booked, invitations issued, etc.

By believing assumptions we can jump to wrongful conclusions that leave us unnecessarily distressed and upset.

Remember this

Evidence must always be factual and not based on negatively biased assumption.

When our mood is low it is very easy to ignore or discount any positive evidence, and this maintains our low mood. CBT won't let you do this. It insists that you review *all* the evidence, looking at both sides of the coin, and then come to a balanced, rather than a biased, conclusion.

Try it now

Look back at some recent negative thoughts about something and pick a strong one. Then ask yourself what evidence you had to *support* it using the criterion above, i.e. would it be accepted by a judge in a court of law? Now imagine that you are the counsel for the defence. Do you have any evidence *against* the truth of this thought? What could you say to support your case that this thought wasn't true?

Writing it all down

You will now be accustomed to using your basic Thought Record (see Chapter 5), so now we'll introduce a new table which has two more columns. Both ask the same thing: 'What evidence do you have to support this view?'. These two extra 'where's the evidence' columns were developed and incorporated into Thought Records by a US clinical psychologist, Christine Padesky, to help her clients construct a more stable, evidence-based challenge to their negative thinking, rather than simply trying to make themselves believe something positive on the basis that it 'sounded right'.

Event	Negative thought(s) and belief strength (%)	Negative feeling(s) and how badly you felt (%)	What evidence do you have to support this thought?	Is there any other way that I can look at this?	What evidence do you have to support this alternative view?	How much do you still believe your initial thoughts? (%). How do you feel now? (%)
Brian calls, yet again, asking to speak to Jane.	Jane is seeing a lot of Brian – she must be having an affair with him (80%)	Devastated (100%) Humiliated (100%)	Lots of contact between Jane and Brian that Jane won't include me in.	While I can't think what else it could be, I have no real facts so perhaps I need to discuss things with Jane in a friendly way.	Jane is always very loving to me at home. She is quite open about seeing Brian so is hardly trying to hide something from me. I know Jane feels very strongly about fidelity in marriage.	Somewhat concerned (20%). Worrying and wondering won't help. I'll chat to Jane and find out what is going on.

The seven-column Thought Record

Action plan: Is there anything you could now do differently to make a difference? Write down any ideas that you have in your workbook.

The first 'Where's the evidence?' column asks you to find evidence to *support* your negative automatic thoughts (NATs) before moving two columns along to find evidence to support your alternative thoughts.

Why do you think the evidence questions are asked this way round? Surely, you might think, the purpose is to prove these thoughts wrong, not try to back them up? But the problem with looking first for evidence to support an alternative view (which you may already have trouble believing) is that it can be too far away from how you presently see things to have any effect.

It is more sensible to see first whether we can find any support for our NATs because:

▶ either we do find some evidence, in which case we may have to accept that, although gloomy or anxiety-provoking, the thoughts' validity means we need to work on either accepting them or changing the root cause

▶ or we have trouble digging up any supporting evidence, which will help us to start weakening the strength of the NAT. No evidence means 'hmmm... perhaps I'm not so certain after all'.

If you believe that you are a bad spouse, for example, you will find it easier to seek out evidence to support that view and then question the validity of that evidence than to search for opposite views. Evidence that you think supports the initial thought might include 'I always seem to be annoyed with my husband/wife', 'I don't spend enough time with him/her', 'Other husbands/wives seem much more loving and relaxed than I am', and so on. When you then move to the alternative view column of your Thought Record to find more optimistic alternatives, you have something to work with. Your alternative thought might be 'I'm not the best spouse in the world but I'm not too bad either' and your evidence to support this view might be 'I only get cross when I'm tired and I always apologize, which my spouse appreciates', or 'This is a very busy period of our lives and we know many couples don't see too much of each other when they are working full time' or 'You never really know as much as you think about other people's relationships. Several of our friends who always seemed very loving have now split up'.

Good evidence requires data, facts and supporting experiences – not just opinions, either yours or anyone else's.

Key idea

The point of thought- and evidence-challenging is not merely to prove our negative thoughts wrong (as they might be right on occasions). Rather, it is to ensure that we have a balanced view rather than a negatively biased view before we take any further action.

Remember this

You will find this easier if you consider both your negative and alternative thoughts as *possibilities* rather than facts. In a sense, you are playing detective – you are asking, if this is so and that is so, then how can...?

Finding evidence for your alternative thinking will be easier when you have worked through the negative evidence columns. For example, imagine your new haircut seems like a disaster when you look in the mirror. Do you have any evidence that this is true (apart from your own opinion)? Even when you don't have any evidence, dredging up an alternative view, such as 'Oh, it's OK', may not have any conviction in it if what you really feel is that you look terrible. This is just self-talk that serves no purpose as it belies your true feelings on the matter.

However, if you ask yourself whether you have any *evidence* that the haircut is OK, you might (perhaps) come up with 'I met my best friend for coffee after my haircut and she said how nice it looked' or 'When I came home tonight, my husband spoke to me for ten minutes and never said a thing, which I regard as quite a positive!'. At the very least, you are starting to shake your conviction that you look atrocious, even if you haven't yet convinced yourself that this is the best haircut ever. In other words, it's a start, and you will be in a better frame of mind than previously.

Try it now

Now practise this. Jot down a few negative thoughts and work on evidence 'for' and 'against' in your Thought Record. As you get used to finding evidence for your thinking, it will loosen your NATs' focus on your mind through tangible, logical argument, rather than simply repeating optimistic alternatives that you don't really feel hold water. This is a very powerful skill.

Key idea

Don't be too hasty. You need to put some effort into finding reliable evidence. Don't simply pay lip service to the process. It is such a valuable skill, it is worth working on and giving time to.

Focusing negatively

It is often much easier to find evidence to support a negative view than it is to find evidence against it. This is due to negative thinking bias (which means that if we feel pessimistic, our thinking leans that way too and doesn't give due credence to alternative views). Evidence to support an alternative view can often be outside of our awareness and you need to search hard for it. Usually what will have happened is that you have discounted it by giving undue weight to your negative thoughts and evidence. One of my clients was describing how depressed she felt because her relationship had broken down and 'everything was wrong with her life'. When I asked about the work promotion (and salary increase) she had recently received, she said, 'Oh, that. It means nothing to me right now.' This is an example of how focusing on the negative aspects of her life precluded this woman from a more balanced view of 'there are some bad things and some good things in it'.

Remember this

Always ask 'What evidence (= actual facts) do I have?'.

As ever, the more you practise, the easier it becomes and the quicker you will begin to feel better about yourself and your own specific difficulties.

Focus points

* You will now understand that looking at a positive alternative to a NAT may not be nearly convincing enough on its own to change your views.
* Looking for evidence to support your NAT often serves to weaken it considerably if your 'evidence' consists only of opinions rather than facts.
* Sometimes you can find evidence to support negative thoughts. But remember, you are not trying to prove your negative thoughts wrong every time but to assess their accuracy and see whether there is an alternative view that stands up to scrutiny.
* While you are learning this new skill, writing things down in a seven-column Thought Record will help you considerably.
* You may need to work quite hard to find evidence to support a more balanced view. If your thinking is very negative, this alternative evidence may be outside of your immediate, pessimistic awareness. If you are focused on your NATs, you will be focused on the evidence that supports them, so challenge your mind to work harder and find other facts or positive events that you may have been discounting.

Rate your effort (1–10) for the exercises you have tried in this chapter ......

Next step

You occasionally hear people talking about 'being in touch with their emotions'. Do you actually know what this means? On other occasions someone might say, 'Oh, I'm just a born worrier' or 'I've been depressed all my life. It's just how I am'. Are our emotions, and the level of them, something we were born with and are stuck with, or is there scope for managing our emotions so that they don't overwhelm us and spoil our life chances? In Chapter 7 you will learn that emotional management can be achieved and how our lives can be the better for it.

Managing your emotions

By the end of this chapter you should:

▶ *be able to appreciate emotions*

▶ *be learning to manage emotions and to keep them appropriate to life situations rather than being overwhelmed by them.*

1 Do you consider yourself to be an emotional person or a rational person?

2 Right now, are you more aware of how you are feeling or what you are thinking?

3 Do you consider yourself to have a predominant mood; for example, are you fairly optimistic or rather pessimistic? Do you remain relaxed when your coping elastic is stretched, or do you start to get anxious or stressed?

4 Do you consider that openly showing emotion is a sign of weakness?

5 When considering how you feel, are you likely to generalize ('I don't feel that great') or to be specific ('I feel very angry')?

Your answers to these questions will give you a good indication of whether and to what extent you are in touch with your emotions: whether you find it easy to state how you feel or whether pinpointing specific emotions – an essential skill if you are to work on changing them – is quite tricky for you. If you find identifying emotions quite difficult, this chapter will show you how to make it easier.

Up to now, we have made a few assumptions about emotions – that you will know what they are and how to identify them. We have focused on how to develop your thought processes by identifying more precisely what is going on in your mind to create feelings that you might find unpleasant or difficult. So let's work more on feelings; our feelings are what drive us and we need the skills to help us develop a 'feel-good' way of being.

Key idea

Keep in the front of your mind what you now understand about the connection between feelings, thoughts and behaviours. Become more curious and interested in the connections you begin to see, as this is a great starting point for change.

Identifying your emotions

While some of my clients say to me 'I've always been a worrier' or 'I cannot recall when I didn't feel depressed', many come to me without realizing that they have had these feelings for years – possibly for as long as they can recall. Because they have never felt any differently, they have (maybe this is you?) assumed that these feelings were 'normal' and not something that could be worked on and changed. Only a serious trauma will have brought them to therapy, and it is then that individuals begin to look at their approach to life events and to see that there is a negative pattern they were unaware of. Someone will mention being 'tired all the time' without realizing that this is an indicator of depression. Or they will feel generally tense and wound-up but fail to appreciate that they don't need to feel this way, the feeling is caused by generalized anxiety that they have not dealt with. They are usually delighted when they learn that what they are suffering from is not difficult to change and can lead to them feeling much better about life.

Remember this

Before you can make changes you need to be able to do two things:

1 be aware of your emotions in general
2 be able to identify the specific emotion(s) for the particular situation you find yourself in.

Try it now

Pay attention to how your body feels right now. Would you say your heart is beating fast or slowly? Is your breathing deep and relaxed or rather shallow? Do you feel either hot or cold? Do you have any other bodily sensations? Do you, for instance, feel full of energy or rather tired? As you read this book you may find yourself feeling quite relaxed (you may be pleased that you are making a start on some self-development) or slightly tense (you may not be certain if this will work or if you will be able to do it correctly). Noticing changes in your body will give you an indication that you are beginning to feel an emotion of some sort.

An awareness of bodily sensations is a good way of working out how you are feeling. Think about some good news you may have had recently. It probably gave your body a feeling of being energized, or perhaps you were able to relax after worrying, or feel a little warm and flushed after a compliment. There may have been an automatic grin and a simple 'feel good' sensation going through you. These are all bodily sensations connected to positive emotion, and they let you know what your feelings are quickly and easily.

Try it now

* Bring to mind two or three recent situations when you have received some good or bad news. For each occasion, write down any thoughts that went through your mind and what physical sensations you remember feeling. What mood was engendered by all this?

* Regularly practise becoming more aware of your feelings at any given time. For example, first thing in the morning and at the end of the day, stop for a moment and ask yourself 'how is my body feeling now?' and 'how am I feeling now?'. Identify the emotion rather than the thought.

Becoming emotionally intelligent

Once you become more aware of your feelings and can identify them *specifically*, you can start to manage them. Managing your emotions is an excellent tool as it helps you to:

▶ stay calm and productive in a crisis, rather than getting over-emotional

▶ connect more with others as you can focus more on their feelings than on your own

▶ stand your ground in the face of adversity rather than running for cover.

It means that your emotions are *appropriate* to a situation rather than *in*appropriate.

This is emotional intelligence, and you may already have heard or read something about this skill. It means being able to identify your emotions correctly and to evaluate the appropriateness of the emotion to the situation. This prevents your emotions from 'running away with you', which can often leave you full of regrets later that you didn't handle the situation as you would have liked

Being specific

We have already mentioned not being too vague about how we feel. However, even if you think you are being specific, you may not be. For example, you might describe yourself as feeling happy. Yet the 'feeling happy' description encompasses a variety of what we might call meta-emotions ('meta-something' meaning a thing that is 'underneath' or 'beyond' something else) – in this case, feeling jolly, playful, jubilant, thrilled, exhilarated, etc. might lie underneath the 'feeling happy' description.

Try it now

Write down some basic emotions such as 'happy', 'angry', 'anxious', 'depressed'. Underneath each of these feelings, write down two or three appropriate meta-emotions. This will help you when you come to pinpointing precisely how you feel about something. Keep your ideas in your workbook and add to them regularly. Not only will this give you a wider range of emotions to use when you label your feelings, but it will also get you more used to expressing and handling emotions, so that identifying them specifically and correctly will become easier for you.

Remember this

To avoid confusion between thoughts and feelings – for example, 'I feel that I'm going to fail this exam' is a thought, despite starting off with an 'I feel' – bear in mind that thoughts are usually expressed in sentences but feelings are usually expressed in single words, e.g. happy, sad, anxious, overwhelmed, etc.

Don't fool yourself

It can be difficult to admit to emotions that make us dislike ourselves. Isn't the purpose of this work to make us feel better about ourselves? How can admitting to feelings such as jealousy or shame help us move forward? Isn't it better to bury such feelings, or relabel them?

Actually, no. What you need to do is to use the skills you have already learned to soften the negative feelings you have about yourself. Instead of telling yourself that admitting to jealousy and shame would make you feel bad about yourself and that you'd rather not, look at things in a different way; for example, 'Most people have negative thoughts and feelings at some point. It just makes me normal.' Or 'It is hard to own up to negative emotions but identifying them honestly is part of my personal development'. Or 'Unless I have the courage to recognize my emotions, I won't be able to change them'.

Key idea

These alternative ways of looking at your problem aren't necessarily positive but they are more balanced and realistic, and they will help you to feel better about yourself.

Is this really how I am feeling?

We have already discussed being honest with yourself. However, even so it is possible to make mistakes that can completely derail your efforts. For the next exercise, instead of searching for a meta-mood, you will use a rating technique to match your mood to your thought. First, read the case study.

Case study

Sherry made her way to the supermarket clutching a detailed list of what she needed. This was an important trip for Sherry. She was about to cook her first meal for her boyfriend's parents and was, naturally, exceedingly anxious that it should go well.

Sherry started walking round with her list clipped to her trolley. Yes, they had this, yes, they had that, but oh, no, they didn't have...! Sherry began to panic slightly. Now she was unprepared. It hadn't occurred to Sherry that some ingredients might not be available so she didn't have a Plan B (give yourself enough time to drive to an alternative supermarket) or a Plan C (adjust or ditch that particular recipe). Why hadn't she planned more carefully? Why hadn't she considered these possibilities and made allowance for them? She was useless. Everything would go wrong now. Paul's parents would consider her a poor girlfriend for their precious son and Paul would be annoyed that Sherry could not get this right. The more Sherry's negative thoughts flooded her brain, the more incapacitated she felt. Her anxiety was rising and her coping skills evaporating. Just as she was trying to compose herself and get her brain back into gear, two small boys raced past and knocked Sherry's trolley sideways. Her list fell to the ground and someone placed a dirty boot print on it. Sherry completely 'lost it'. She turned to the mother of the young boys and angrily berated her for not having more control over them. Sherry was literally shaking with anger. A passing assistant offered to help and led Sherry to a chair so she could sit down for a moment to compose herself. Meanwhile the store assistant found her shopping list and cleaned it up. As she sat there, Sherry felt mortified. Why had she got so angry? They were just little boys. It wasn't the end of the world. Did she have anger management issues that she wasn't aware of and needed to address – on top of everything else?'

Reading this, what would you say was Sherry's driving emotion? Was it anger? Was it frustration or intolerance? What was really going on? We'll set this out as a Thought Record (note: Thought Records don't have to be in a 'column' format. You can use a more informal – and possibly clearer – approach as shown below).

Situation: Food shopping. Find the store doesn't have the ingredients I need, followed by children being allowed to run wild through the store and tip over my trolley.

Thoughts:	How useless I am not to have planned for such an eventuality and have a Plan B (90%)
	How can a mother let her children behave in such an appalling way – there's no discipline at all these days (80%)
	This meal is so important but it's going to be a disaster now (100%)
Emotions:	anger (70%), frustration (50%), distress (80%), high anxiety (100%)

By setting the problem out in this way we can see much more clearly:

▶ what Sherry's motivating thoughts were

▶ what Sherry's exact emotions were

▶ the strength of these emotions.

It becomes clear that, although Sherry initially felt that it was her anger that had got the better of her, it was actually her high anxiety levels that triggered her self-critical thoughts and angry outburst. Sherry was more anxious about her abilities as a cook than she was concerned by poor, childish behaviour.

Key idea

You can see that by rating Sherry's thoughts and emotions, it was easy to make a link between what was really bothering her and the emotion (high anxiety) that she needed to deal with. This is a vital discovery. Sherry needed to appreciate that she was being driven by high anxiety in order to be able to work to reduce it (and, by doing so, save the day regarding the dinner party). Had Sherry erroneously continued to berate herself for her anger (her secondary or meta-emotion), she would have drawn a blank as to what was really needed: an exercise in constructive thinking about alternatives and more optimistic thoughts about how the meal might go to reduce her anxiety levels.

Remember this

Use a Thought Record to help you to identify your driving emotion. Don't get side-tracked either by meta-emotions or by failing to be completely honest with yourself. Practise the skill of rating thoughts and emotions to get the strongest and best match.

Focus points

* You have learned skills in this chapter to help you to identify your emotions more easily. You can do this by becoming aware of physical sensations relating to your mood, by becoming more familiar with the wide variety of emotions so that it is easier for you to select the correct one and by being specific rather than general.

* We have restressed the importance of matching your mood to your emotion and this can be done by using a Thought Record to rate your thoughts and feelings and to discover which is the strongest – which has the highest rating.

* You may also have discovered that the emotion you initially pinpoint turns out to be a red herring when you use your ratings technique.

* Always be honest with yourself about how you feel or you will not be able to make effective changes.

* Practise 'collecting' moods – it is interesting as well as helpful!

Rate your effort (1–10) for the exercises you have tried in this chapter ......

Next step

As we said quite forcefully at the end of Chapter 2 on goal-setting, nothing happens without ACTION! In that context, we were referring to positive action, something that will move you

forward and be a motivating presence. In Chapter 8 we will look at the double-edged sword of our varied behaviours: how action, if it is not appropriate to the solution of the problem, can be a maintaining factor and keep our problems going. In this context, inaction can be an action, i.e. it is an informed decision to do nothing. Chapter 8 will help you through the minefield of constructing useful behavioural patterns that are helpful, rather than destructive behavioural patterns that keep you locked within your difficulties.

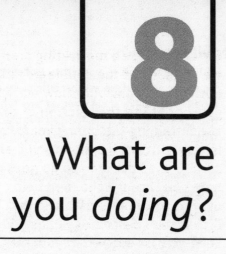

What are you *doing*?

Our behavioural responses seem to come naturally to us and we rarely question whether we might have done something different. When life is going well, this is fine, but when things become difficult our behaviour might be a contributory cause without our realizing it. By the end of this chapter you should:

▶ *understand the importance of behaviour in helping you to think more optimistically and to feel better*

▶ *be able to use behaviour as a tool for positive progress.*

I hope that you will have found it straightforward to come up with five different skills and concepts. If not, examine why – did you skip a chapter because you thought it not relevant? Did you feel that there wasn't a skill or technique that would be of use to you? Or did you get muddled and found it hard to think of something? If so, review the first few chapters and find at least one skill from each chapter that might be useful to you.

Some of the ideas you may have noted might include:

▶ understanding the connection between thoughts, feelings and behaviours

▶ knowing how to use conceptualization to assess accurately what is going on

▶ knowing how to work out which thought is the most important to you in relation to the emotions it gives rise to

▶ how to use a Thought Record

▶ how to replace negative thinking with more balanced, re-evaluative thoughts

- how to check for evidence to support these alternative thoughts

- how to identify emotions

- how to work out the correct emotion that links to your strongest thought

- and perhaps more specific and detailed breakdowns of the above.

The role of behaviour

So far we have given little attention to the role that our behaviour plays in what we think and how we feel. Now we shall take a detailed look at behaviour, to understand the very powerful effect that this has on outcomes, and how it may reinforce negative views.

Look back at any conceptualizations that you have drawn up (or use the example in this book) and notice what the impact was of how you acted on maintaining (or getting rid of) your problem(s).

Key idea

When our behaviour has clearly kept a problem going, we look at this as part of the problem – it is negative or self-defeating behaviour, rather than rational or action-oriented behaviour.

Let's take the example of Peter, who fears that he is dull and boring. He is invited to a party. His thoughts are likely to be along the lines of: 'What's the point of going along. No one will want to talk to me.' Or 'Even when I make an effort, all I can think of is that the person listening is wondering how soon they can get away from me and find someone interesting. It's very demoralizing.'

In this state of negative thinking, what is Peter's most likely *behavioural* response? The likelihood is that his *behaviour* will mirror his *thinking*. In this case:

- he may turn down all social invitations

- he may accept invitations but avoid getting involved in conversations which will show up how 'boring' he is

- he may stand in a corner, avoid eye contact and leave early (telling himself 'at least I went along').

Are these behaviours helpful to Peter? He might say that they are, as they help him to manage his anxiety and to avoid putting himself in stressful situations. Although this is certainly true, if Peter would like to improve his social life and status and is unhappy with the (possibly erroneous) idea that he is dull and boring, then his behaviours are very unhelpful. They simply confirm to him what he already thought:

▶ that he is better staying away from social occasions

▶ that even if he makes an effort, it ends in failure.

Behavioural change

Although it seems simplistic to say that if you can see that your behaviour leads to negative outcomes, then you should change your behaviour, this is the basic principle underlying this aspect of CBT!

But however obvious this seems, most people have problems working out what they could do differently and how they can be sure that these changes will help, i.e. an unwillingness to take a risk without a cast-iron guarantee about its effect. Herein lies a dilemma for many folk, as we cannot know for certain what the outcome of a new behaviour might be.

We *have* to be willing to take the risk, first a little by working out what alternative behaviours we could use in a specific situation and what is the likelihood of a different (better) outcome. We then experiment – we try out our new idea or ideas in the hope that they will be helpful, and we see what happens. Once we have assessed the new outcome, we can either decide to keep practising the new behaviour or go back to the drawing board and take another look at the situation.

Key idea

Think about new behavioural strategies as experiments. Give yourself confidence by being open-minded about the outcome. You are not necessarily looking to prove that what you were thinking or doing previously was wrong but rather to test the validity of your thoughts, to observe and weigh up any new outcomes to see if they are preferable to the old outcomes, and also – in the case of anxiety – to learn to become confident through exposure to feared situations, rather than avoiding them.

THE ALTERNATIVES

If we accept the CBT premise that some type of change is required to help us move forward, what options do we have?

Try it now

Before reading on, think about possible options. There are three clear, general options. What might they be?

Keeping in mind that your goal for each of the options below is to feel better – to experience more optimistic emotions – you can consider:

▶ adjusting your thinking about the situation. Would looking at things from a different, more balanced perspective be helpful and make you feel better?

▶ doing something differently. If what we are doing now isn't working very well for us, it might pay us to take a different approach and see if we get a better outcome

▶ accepting the way things are now. This is a strong decision in itself and an option many decide to choose. Change is a balance, and sometimes we realize that there is a cost/benefit scale in place – once we contemplate change, we realize that the disadvantages outweigh the advantages. The change required might simply be too much for you just now. If this is the case, there is nothing wrong with that as long as it is an informed decision. Coming to terms with things as they are can be a positive way forward in itself.

GUIDED DISCOVERY

The American CBT therapist Christine Padesky coined the term 'guided discovery' for behavioural experimenting. Guided discovery means trying something new without any preconceived ideas about how things should turn out. We are just testing our thinking and our behaviours by trying something out to see what happens. We always discover something. It may be that what we found out wasn't helpful, but at least we know not to try that again. Or we discover that something we might not have thought of before has amazingly positive results and we decide to continue with this new, helpful way forward.

Remember this

The main point is that at the start of the experiment we don't have any certainty about the outcome but we do have some hopes for its success. Some of you may know this as 'managed risk', i.e. although things could go wrong, we are reasonably confident that they won't, or that we can manage them if they do.

THE SELF-FULFILLING PROPHECY

This common expression derives from a 'what you think or what you do decides what will happen' school of thought. Where your thoughts and behaviours are negative, the chances are that the outcome will be negative.

Case study

Jean grew up in a family where, loved though she was, the mantra was always 'could do better'. If you got 60 per cent, you could have achieved 70 per cent; if you got 70 per cent, then 80 per cent would have been better, and so on. Jean, not unnaturally, developed an 'I'm not good enough' belief that followed her into adulthood and the world of work. Although very competent at her job, every time a promotional possibility loomed, Jean shied away from it. When asked by co-workers why she did not apply, her answer was always the same: 'I'd only mess up and then I'd be out of a job completely. Best to stay where I am'. Jean's view was that if you didn't try then you couldn't fail. The idea that she might not fail but actually succeed, or that if she did fail it wouldn't be the end of the world, never occurred to her. Better to do nothing at all than to do something that didn't work out well was Jean's attitude to all aspects of her life. Better to turn down a potential date than accept it and possibly be rejected. Better not to accept an invitation to play tennis than to go along and have people snigger at how bad you were. Although this way of thinking and behaving (even lack of action is a form of behaviour) kept Jean 'safe', it also stoked the fuels of her 'I'm no good at anything' belief, and Jean missed out on dozens of pleasant life experiences because of it.

Avoidance and *escape* work very well for Jean, but they maintain her problem. Jean's actions (or inactions) simply confirm her view of herself as someone who is never good enough. Jean never learns that she might easily handle a job promotion and that it would open up her life. Or that accepting an invitation might be the first step in finding a life partner – or at least a tennis partner. By risking nothing, Jean is trapped in her limited life, which in turn reinforces her 'I'm not good enough for better' views. She never tests it out.

A BEHAVIOURAL EXPERIMENT

You have put Thought Records to good use so far and here is something similar. This Thought Record is specifically for recording behavioural experiments and their outcomes. It offers you a good step-by-step approach to this.

We'll take the case of Jean as an example and look at what she might do to make changes.

What are you going to try?	What do you predict will happen and how will you feel? (%)	What actually happened?	What have you learned from this?	How can you build on this?
I am going to apply for a promotion that is probably well within my capabilities.	I will either be rejected outright or, worse, I will get the job and will mess it up. I will feel anxious (80%), humiliated (70%) and hopeless (90%).	I was encouraged by how well my work is viewed. I was actually told that I could do better than this particular job and that my employer would like to train me for something more interesting.	I was very anxious at the interview, but less than I expected (about 60%). Hearing how well my employer thought of me gave me confidence. I am considering their offer. Instead of feeling hopeless I felt confident (50%).	I can risk taking the new job training. I can start to take a few other risks as well – my view that things will always turn out badly isn't proving correct so I will keep trying.

'Behavioural Experiment' Thought Record

In the example given, Jean decides to risk an internal job application. It is nerve-racking for her, and she has no real idea what the result will be. Her prediction of the outcome is very negative. But she gives it a try, and afterwards evaluates what actually happened compared to her prediction of what would happen. In Jean's case, she discovered that things turned out much better than she had expected, and she was able to learn from this and build on it.

SAFETY-SEEKING BEHAVIOURS

Think about any difficulties you have that seem hard to change. If, for example, you suffer from generalized anxiety, you may be too nervous to try things that seem difficult to achieve and/ or that would be embarrassing if you failed. You will have a negative view of what the outcome is likely to be – which is possibly a faulty view or perhaps because of a previous bad experience – so the safest thing to you is to stay safe and not attempt things that might go horribly wrong. Sometimes people have such thoughts even when they have no experience at all of disaster; they simply have a negative thinking bias. Consequently they never find out that either things don't turn out as badly as expected, or that they have more resources to cope then they had realized.

The saddest part of 'staying safe' is that your brain becomes trained to think that you are coping well with a dangerous situation. You therefore not only maintain the problem, you compound it. The less we do something, the less confident we become that we could attempt it. Sooner or later, our nervousness about getting on aeroplanes becomes nervousness about any sort of public transport. Our worries about being dull and boring at parties descends into never accepting invitations.

We call these sort of avoidances 'safety-seeking behaviours'. This is because your clear goal, as a sensible and intelligent person, is to keep yourself (and/or others, perhaps) safe from possible harm. Safety behaviours therefore seem eminently sensible. Surely 'staying safe' is an important and vital goal that supersedes all others? Well, yes, but the mistake we make when we avoid something rather than going ahead with it is that of *assuming* that we are heading for danger. It never occurs to many people that these safety behaviours, often time-consuming and certainly limiting, could be a waste of time and effort. All those opportunities missed! All those possible successes passed by. What a shame!

What is needed to change things? Firstly, you have to decide how you would like things to be different. A problem is only a problem if it bothers you. Perhaps you enjoy staying at home alone or don't mind never going to the sports club, or on a train, or trying for promotion. In that case you have no problem. However, if you wish things were different, then it is a problem.

GRADED EXPOSURE

You are now an experienced goal-setter and your first task is to set your goal. What would you like to test out? However, before setting up a behaviour experiment it is important that you understand the principle of 'graded exposure'. While some people are willing to dive in at the deep end of the pool to learn to swim, most prefer to take smaller steps, such as paddling in the shallow end, first. We call this 'graded exposure'; it is like going up a series of small steps and seeing how you get on at the first step before climbing on to the next. The majority of people prefer this method of behavioural testing!

Testing things out

In your workbook, draw up a 'Behavioural Experiment' Thought Record like the one above. Write down in the first column one or two things you might try that will stretch you a little. For example, if you suffer from social shyness, decide to speak to a shop assistant and/or to smile at the person next to you in the cappuccino queue. Be curious about what happens.

Try it now

You need to try something that is not radically different from your more negative behaviour but which is a good 'first step'. Once you are comfortable with the first step, you can take another step, and then another, towards your final goal. Think in terms of pushing yourself just a little beyond your comfort zone on this occasion.

Key idea

It is vital to be organized and to decide first on your graded plan of action. Don't just 'give things a go', but write out first every single step you plan to take. Never move on a step until you are entirely comfortable with the exposure you have already tried. Once you feel relaxed, move out of your comfort zone into creating a new one.

Once you have decided what you are prepared to try, ask yourself 'What is the worst thing that can happen?'. Write this down. When I ask this question of clients frightened of adjusting their behaviours, they will often say 'I really don't know – I have never thought that far'. They are responding to 'gut feelings' that tell them something bad will happen, but they have never been brave enough to think about exactly what that 'something bad' might be and how they might handle it.

For example, if you consider yourself dull and boring, you might become anxious if invited to a get-together of some sort. While your negative predictions may run along the lines of 'People will find me dull. It will be a dreadful evening', ask yourself as well, 'What would be the worst thing about this?'. Your answer might be 'I have such low self-esteem anyway that I may never go out again after a bad evening socially'.

A very negative prediction. But it might not be true and your experiment will give you the chance to find out.

Now, using graded exposure, decide on an experiment. For example, if you are nervous about confronting a work colleague over some contentious issues, you might decide to pick just one issue (an 'easier to resolve' issue, perhaps) and consider, for a 'first step', finding a time to approach him/her when he/she is not going to be especially stressed. Advance planning will help you. Decide ahead of time how you might tackle the problem in the best way, and then be willing to test it out.

DROP YOUR SAFETY BEHAVIOURS

You now understand what safety behaviours are. When you are concerned about being considered dull at a party, your safety behaviours might be to avoid too much eye contact so that people won't talk to you, or to find an excuse to leave early. When you are confronting a colleague, you might decide to hide behind an email rather than engage in a face-to-face discussion, or you may keep prevaricating and finding reasons why 'the timing isn't right'. As we have already seen, safety behaviours maintain problems rather than overcoming them, so decide what avoidant behaviours you use, and determine to drop them for this experiment.

For some people, the mere mention of testing out something that seems fearful is too much. Don't worry, there is another good way to start and that is by imagining yourself in the new situation. I have used this method with many clients, who sit in my office, close their eyes and picture themselves getting into a lift, or driving on a motorway, or speaking to a stranger. I encourage them to note their surroundings, what else is going on, and how they feel. For many people, even imagining the situation they fear makes them feel very anxious at first. But eventually they find that they can picture themselves doing this new thing without their initial stomach-churning reaction. They begin to feel familiar with the idea and with the good outcome. At this point, most are willing to try out the new behaviour 'on the street', and they move on well from there. So do consider this method as a useful first step in your behavioural testing.

Now you need to become pro-active. But do remember, your 'first step' goal is flexible. If you find, after taking the steps above, that it still seems too difficult, then cut your first step in half to something more manageable; for example, 'I really don't think I can stay at the party for two hours after all, but I will stay for an hour on this occasion and longer next time'. But remember, this is about *doing* something, not considering or wondering about doing it. It means trying something different to see if you can get a better result. It means challenging negative assumptions and predictions to test their validity. It means identifying self-defeating behaviour and seeing whether there isn't a better way – a way to make you feel better, to lift your spirits, to give you more confidence.

Try it now

Build 'prediction testing' into your everyday life. Each evening, think of something that you might consider would have a negative outcome the next day and test this out. It can be as simple as baking a cake if your normal view would be along the lines of 'I'm a hopeless cook'. Get used to the idea of challenging preconceptions. Be curious about what happens. You might bake a super cake and decide to try again next week. Or it may be awful and you decide your original view was correct – even a negative result is of interest – and you can evaluate whether you need to accept things as they are or find another way of tackling things.

Use your 'Behavioural Experiment' Thought Record to do this. Have an open mind. Be genuinely curious about the results. When they are positive, determine to continue with them rather than reverting to self-defeating ways.

Focus points

✻ You will now understand more about the huge influence that behaviour has on what we think and how we feel.

✻ You can recognize self-defeating behaviour (i.e. behaviour that maintains a problem) and also identify safety-seeking behaviours that seem to help you feel better at the time but don't reduce the problem in any way.

✻ Using behavioural experiments is an excellent way of trying new behaviours in a controlled way so that you set yourself up to succeed rather than to fail, to discover something positive rather than to be disappointed.

✻ You can draw on some of the skills you have learned in earlier chapters, such as goal-setting and searching for evidence, to help you conduct these experiments. You can build on your learning by designing new experiments that are based on your discoveries in previous ones.

Rate your effort (1–10) for the exercises you have tried in this chapter ......

Next step

You now have a grasp of what we call 'event-specific' thoughts and how they can affect how we feel and what we do. But what happens when none of this seems to work? When our negative beliefs seem so strong and so cast in concrete that there's just no budging them, however hard we try? The answer is that we can learn further skills that will help us to dislodge thoughts and beliefs even when they don't appear that way to us; they appear to be facts and truths – and you can't argue with facts and truths. But are they facts and truths? And can we argue with them and shift them? Yes we can, and you will learn how in Chapter 9.

What drives our thinking?

By the end of this chapter you will be able to:

▶ *understand clearly the differences and links between thoughts, assumptions and beliefs*

▶ *start to use skills that will enable you to replace old, unhelpful beliefs with new, more helpful ones.*

?   **Self-assessment**

1 Have you found thought-challenging easy and helpful, or has it been an uphill struggle?

2 When you debate with friends, do you find yourself arguing your corner quite strongly, determined that they should come round to your way of thinking?

3 Do you notice yourself validating beliefs that were held by your parents?

4 In general, do the personal beliefs that you hold about yourself help you in life or hold you back?

5 Can you identify any strong belief you have now which developed from a negative personal experience?

If you have answered 'yes' to most or all of these questions you have a strong belief system. Where these beliefs are positive they will enhance your life but where they are negative they may diminish it. The problem with beliefs is that we tend to view them as facts and rarely question them. To help you become more optimistic and open-minded, you need to learn how you can chip away at even the strongest beliefs and refine them or replace them with beliefs that will be more helpful to you. If you answered 'no' to these questions, you may not need to read this chapter except out of curiosity!

The difference between thoughts and beliefs

So far we have focused on the idea that our thoughts decide how we feel. Hopefully this makes enough sense to you and you understand it well enough to be able now to accept a new concept.

What we will do now is to explore deeper layers of thinking that will help you account for why automatic thoughts are not always easy to challenge and dismiss. When newly developed optimistic thinking to counteract NATs (such as 'People spoke to me at the party so I must be reasonably interesting') flies in the face of deeply held and often intractable beliefs (such as 'I've been dull and boring all my life'), it makes little progress. This is why some people have difficulty making thinking shifts of a meaningful nature by using only event-specific negative automatic thoughts (NATs) and need to work on their core beliefs.

Firstly, recognizing negative thinking and self-defeating behaviours are unquestionably an essential starting point for making changes. In fact, for many people – perhaps for some readers of this book – these skills may be *all* you need to help you cope with your problems effectively. But for many people, no matter how diligently they work on these skills and techniques, they find their thoughts hard to shift and their emotions remain very negative. The beauty of CBT is that it is able to accommodate this difficulty by helping you to look at the deeper layers of thinking that we refer to as assumptions and beliefs and which may be helping to trap your thinking in negative mode.

To put this in simple terms, we have three levels of thinking:

▶ automatic thoughts (our top layer of thinking)

▶ assumptions (our middle layer of thinking)

▶ beliefs (our bottom layer of thinking).

AUTOMATIC THOUGHTS

You've already read about these, so here we will just put them into context.

These are our 'chatterbox' thoughts. They are day-to-day thoughts which, as you already know, can be positive, negative or neutral. These thoughts tend to be 'event specific', i.e. they come about as a reaction to something that happens. For example, if you are driving and someone cuts in front of you, you might feel angry and think how rude drivers are these days, or you might feel worried and think that driving is becoming very unsafe with so many cars on the road. In either case, the event has caused the thought and the feeling. The 'event' can be as simple as watching TV or reading a book. It doesn't have to be momentous but *something* will cause a thought to pop into your mind to which you then react emotionally.

BELIEFS

Beliefs are our 'bottom layer' of thinking, but it is our beliefs that drive our assumptions. Assumptions are rather like branches attached to a tree trunk. So it makes sense to look at the tree (beliefs) before the branch (assumptions). We will return to assumptions later in the chapter.

The great power of beliefs is that they are not necessarily triggered by a specific event (although they might be), but lie deep within us, absolute and unchanging. Beliefs often develop in childhood, when we are very influenced by the beliefs and actions of others, especially our immediate family. Think of the effect on your beliefs about religion if you grew up in a religious family, for example. While they might be different for each individual, you would almost certainly hold strong religious (or possibly anti-religious) beliefs after growing up in this environment. Or how would you feel about yourself if your parents were very critical of you as a child? You might develop a belief that nothing you did was ever good enough, perhaps. So upbringing plays a great part in shaping our beliefs about ourselves and our world.

Beliefs can also develop from events that have great impact on us either as a child (being frightened by a dog, for example, might generate a life-long view of dogs as dangerous) or in our early adulthood (being rejected by someone you love might give rise to an 'I'm unlovable' belief). Often, these beliefs are confirmed by 'proof'; you read in the paper about a dog attacking someone, which confirms your 'dogs are dangerous' belief' or your failure to get a job promotion confirms your 'I'm not good enough' belief.

It is when you learn to identify NATs that you begin to see patterns of thinking developing and you should to be curious about these. For example, if you shy away from challenges because of views such as 'I'll be no good at it so best not to embarrass myself', or 'I'll let someone else do that, they'll be far better than me', then those thoughts provide information about something you believe about yourself. In this instance it might be an 'I'm a failure' belief.

Key idea

Beliefs are so basic and solid that we can misinterpret them as truths and facts. It never occurs to us to question them.

Different types of belief

Our beliefs, generally, divide themselves into four basic types.

► Ourselves ('I am unattractive')

► Others ('people can't be trusted')

► The world ('the world is a dangerous place')

► The future ('things can only get worse')

We are far more likely to re-evaluate our thinking than our beliefs. This is because beliefs, in our minds, tend to equal 'truths'. So we fail to give beliefs the attention they deserve by questioning them and challenging their validity – and they continue to generate our negative thinking in any or all of the areas mentioned above.

Try it now

Think of and write down at least one example of a negative belief you hold that falls into each of the above categories.

If you found that difficult, here are some examples

Possible beliefs about ourselves:

► I'm shy

► I'm selfish

- I'm dull
- I'm anti-social
- I'm as thick as two short planks
- I have a dreadful figure

About others:

- People are so selfish these days
- No one helps you on in life
- Other people are only interested in themselves
- Traffic wardens take a real delight in giving you a ticket
- Nobody cares about me

About the world:

- The world outside is full of danger for most people
- The world only favours those who are ruthless
- The world is very war-like

About the future

- There is no hope ahead of us
- Nothing will ever change for the better
- I will always feel this way

Now be brave and honest and tick any of the above that rings a bell in your own mind. It's OK – most of us share some of these views. But views they are: not facts, although we tend to treat them as though they are. The 'if I think it, it must be so' activation!

AWAKENING OUR BELIEFS

We rarely give much thought to our beliefs, even when they are activated. Realizing the power of long-held beliefs over our present thinking patterns is a very important step in making changes to a more realistic and optimistic way of looking at life.

For example, someone with an 'I'm unlikeable' belief will be devastated if a stranger they meet at a party takes little interest in them. Instead of appreciating that they had little in common with each other and that this sort of thing often happens, that person's thinking is more likely to run along the lines of 'I cannot seem to make friends no matter how hard I try' or 'There's obviously something wrong with me that drives people away'.

Assumptions

Assumptions are the link between our day-to-day NATs and our beliefs. Assumptions also create what we might call our 'rules for living', i.e. the things we feel that we need to do in order to survive. The way we go about our daily lives is heavily influenced by our beliefs and assumptions.

For example, a person holding the negative *belief* that they are a worthless person may make the *assumption* that 'if I apply for a promotion at work I know I won't get it'.

You can see how the *belief* activates the *assumption*. The assumption in turn activates a *rule for living* that this person feels they are right to follow: 'If I don't apply for better jobs I'll protect myself from the pain of rejection.' Or you may develop a rule for living not to socialize, as you consider this will prevent your 'I am boring' belief being put to the test.

Try it now

Identify some rules for living of your own. We all have them. For instance, one of mine is: 'If I am nice to people, they will like me.' Someone else might have as a rule for living: 'If I am nice to people, they will take advantage of me.' Write down a few of your own rules, then see if you can identify any assumptions or beliefs that might have given rise to these rules. (If this is difficult, read through the rest of this chapter and come back to this.)

Remember this

Assumptions and rules for living tend to blur into one another so don't worry too much about the distinction – what is more important is that you understand how they are activated by beliefs and are the cause of our specific thinking styles.

One way to recognize assumptions is their tendency to have an 'If… then…' element to them, such as:

▶ '*If* I don't meet the work deadline *then* I'm sure to be demoted.'

▶ '*If* I open my heart to him *then* I am sure to get hurt.'

▶ '*If* I don't help the children with their homework *then* I'm a bad mother.'

The links with negativity

Let's use a case study to put these concepts into context.

Case study

Susan was a young actress who loved her work and her family. She was also engaged to a wonderful young man who she considered to be the love of her life.

Yet within a few weeks of Susan reflecting on how happy and complete her life was, her beloved father died and her fiancé broke the news to her that he was in love with someone else and was breaking off the engagement.

Susan's world collapsed. Not only did she have to face the future alone without the two men she had loved best, but she was also left with a real sense of abandonment. She developed understandable beliefs that love didn't last and that losing love created unbearable pain. In trying to get herself and her life back together, Susan developed an assumption that the more you loved someone the more you were exposed to being abandoned and let down. From this she developed a rule for living that if you didn't give your heart fully away to anyone, you would keep yourself free of this type of suffering.

Susan remained single rather than even attempt to develop other loving relationships and she also kept herself distant from friends and family, as getting too close always activated her 'you will abandon me sooner or later' belief. Susan's training as an actress helped her to present herself as charming and articulate while at the same time ensuring that she didn't connect closely with anyone at all.

We can formulate Susan's problems in this way:

▶ Susan's early life experiences

▶ the beliefs she developed from these

▶ the assumptions that these beliefs engendered

▶ the events that activated Susan's beliefs and assumptions, her NATs and negative behaviours.

Susan's early life experiences
The two men who meant the most to Susan both abandoned her, one through death and the other through betrayal.

Susan's beliefs
No matter how dearly you love someone, they will abandon you eventually.

Susan's assumptions and 'rules for living'
Assumption: if you lose someone you love, the pain is unbearable.
Rule for living: never truly give your heart to someone as they are likely to break it.

Trigger events that cause Susan's assumptions and rules to be activated
Anyone, especially men, trying to forge a close relationship with Susan.

Negative thoughts and behaviours that maintain Susan's problem
Thoughts: even though I meet some charming men, I cannot risk being hurt and abandoned as the pain would be too great.

Behaviours: Susan never becomes fully engaged mentally or emotionally with others (leading to distance and loneliness as a consequence).

Source: Adapted from Beck, Cognitive Therapy: The Basics and Beyond

---

Try it now

Using the model above, see if you can make a case study of any negative beliefs and assumptions that you have that might be triggering negative thinking. Write down the headings above and write at least one sentence that is personal to your own background, thoughts and beliefs under each one.

The purpose of understanding how beliefs and assumptions give rise to negative thinking is that, once you have identified beliefs that hold you back, you can learn how to replace them with more realistic beliefs that will be more helpful to you.

Uncovering your beliefs

It isn't too difficult to uncover personal beliefs. What tends to be harder is questioning their validity and seeing them in a new light, as opinions and not truths. After all, your mind has considered these beliefs to be truths for a long time.

Try it now

If your beliefs don't jump off the page at you, then you need to start by looking for any patterns in your NATs (this is another good reason for keeping written records of your thought processes). Do you see any patterns? Does any particular belief come to mind? Keep looking – there will be something. You may be able to make quite a list of beliefs.

Next, look back at your past experiences for clues to how you came to think this way. Jot these down – don't try to keep everything in your head – and gradually formulate a set of negative beliefs that make sense to you in the context of what might be maintaining your negative thinking and behaviours. You might like to set your ideas out under headings such as these:

* Patterns of negative thinking
* Likely belief(s) that have activated these thoughts
* Past experiences that might have formulated such beliefs.

Things should start making sense to you now.

In our case study, Susan was able to track her 'people you love abandon you' beliefs.

Key idea

We are less aware of our negative beliefs than we are of our negative thinking. This is because we convince ourselves that our beliefs are 'truths'. Constantly remind yourself that negative beliefs are no more than a point of view and that they may not be true at all, no matter how strongly you believe them.

REMEMBER THE DOWNWARD ARROW?

You learned this technique in Chapter 4. The Downward Arrow is also extremely useful in uncovering beliefs. For this purpose, you adjust the question from 'What does this mean to me?' to 'What does this say about me/others/the world/the future?'.

Here's an example.

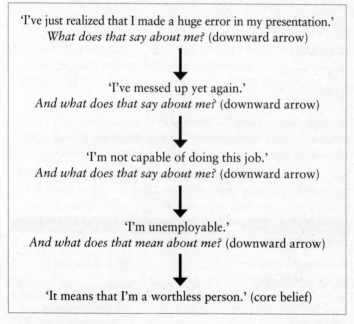

'I've just realized that I made a huge error in my presentation.'
What does that say about me? (downward arrow)

'I've messed up yet again.'
And what does that say about me? (downward arrow)

'I'm not capable of doing this job.'
And what does that say about me? (downward arrow)

'I'm unemployable.'
And what does that mean about me? (downward arrow)

'It means that I'm a worthless person.' (core belief)

REMEMBER RATINGS?

Your earlier learning is now starting to serve a practical use. Here is another excellent use of ratings. Look at your list of negative beliefs (or compile one if you haven't already done so) and give each of the beliefs a priority rating, i.e. ask yourself:

▶ to what extent each belief bothers you

▶ what negative effect each belief has on you.

The purpose of this is to avoid you spending time and energy on beliefs that you can live with. Spend your time on those beliefs that have a high rating. Alternatively (or in addition) you can divide your beliefs into different categories: those that need immediate attention, those that might need some work in the future, and those that don't warrant much attention at the moment.

Challenging beliefs

For some people, thought-challenging is enough to shift beliefs as well as thoughts, so the whole process of change can be quite fast. However, where beliefs are deeply held and have been held for a long time, they might be harder to change. Thought-challenging won't be powerful enough to shift them, as the beliefs will override attempts to re-evaluate the thoughts. In such a case, you will need to work on the belief, rather than the thoughts.

Belief change requires different techniques to thought-challenging and – be warned – it can take longer. (Think how embedded some of your beliefs are.)

Your core beliefs will drive your assumptions, which in turn create your rules for living. For example:

My belief	Assumptions	My rules for living
Others aren't to be trusted.	If I put my faith in anybody, they'll let me down.	Always assume that others will let you down, so never be dependent on anyone.
I'm physically unattractive.	Others must look at me with ridicule or pity.	Stay at home rather than going out. Dress in a way that draws little attention to myself.
I must do everything perfectly.	Unless what I do is perfect, I'm a failure.	Keep going over and over things until I'm certain I've done the best that I can, even where this takes hours of my time.

The basic goal of adjusting beliefs is the same as for adjusting thoughts – it involves weakening and loosening old beliefs and strengthening new, more helpful beliefs. There are a variety of techniques that can help you to achieve this. Try them all – you may find that some work better for you than others.

Try it now

This skill involves drawing a straight line on a piece of paper and filling it in as follows. First, select a negative belief. For example, 'I am a horrible person'. Now look at the continuum below:

Jack the Ripper				Mother Teresa
0%	25%	50%	75%	100%

X

Now think about where, in this context, you might place two or three people you know: for example, your father, your best friend, your worst enemy. Now where would you place yourself?

What do you make of this? What does it tell you about the validity of your belief?

Ask yourself what *advantages* there are in hanging on to your old belief. Then ask yourself what are the *disadvantages* of continuing to hold such beliefs. Surprisingly, for some people, there can be benefits in holding on to a negative belief. For example, believing that you aren't a very capable person can help ensure that family, friends, etc. do a lot for you. On a lighter note, believing that you can't cook means you never have to entertain (or perhaps your partner takes this chore on instead of you). What I call 'learned helplessness' is something I have seen in several clients over the years.

Working in this way can help to loosen the idea that your negative belief(s) are helpful and encourage you to look at things with a wider perspective.

Key idea

You are not trying to make yourself believe that something is true or not; you are simply considering what, on balance, is the most useful belief.

In Chapter 8 you learned how to set up behavioural experiments to test the validity of your thoughts. You can use exactly the same skill to test your old and new beliefs.

Try it now

Using the same Behavioural Experiment Thought Record that you used in Chapter 8, write down your negative belief and describe a way that you might test out its validity. When you have actually carried it out, look at what you have learned from the experiment.

Remember this

Beliefs are usually no more than thinking habits. If we have come to a specific (but possibly erroneous) conclusion a long time ago, we tend to let the belief hang around until it is habitual. Often it is nothing more than a habit.

Creating more helpful beliefs

As with negative thoughts, shaking off a negative belief is only one side of the coin. You also need to know how to develop some alternative, more optimistic and helpful beliefs in their place.

A simple way to start this process is to write down on the left-hand side of a piece of paper the negative beliefs you have identified. On the right-side of the page, write down some more balanced alternatives. This may be quite easy for you – it could just be something you have never done before and once you start you may see your negative beliefs disappear quite quickly. As always, ensure that your newer belief isn't too ridiculously positive; it has to be believable to you as you think about it as a possible alternative.

If, for example, your old, negative belief is 'I have nothing to say to people', your new, more helpful belief might be 'I can chat on a one-to-one basis and I am a good listener'.

Here are some examples of this.

My old beliefs	More balanced alternatives
'Nobody likes me.'	'No one is liked by everyone so it is natural that some people won't like me while others do. (I think Jim likes me.)'
'I'm not good at anything.'	'There are lots of things I can't do (which makes me about the same as everyone else) but I can ride a bike, change a fuse and cook sausages for a start. Now, what else...?'
'My boyfriend has left me. I'm obviously not a lovable person.'	'As I write this, beautiful film stars, gorgeous men and women, are being told by someone they love that their relationship is over. This happens. We aren't unlovable people, just not a good fit with that particular person.'

The purpose of doing this is not to get rid of these assumptions – you can see from the above that none of the alternatives absolutely deny the original belief – but to start loosening them. They will then gradually disappear on their own.

BIN 'SHOULD', 'MUST' AND 'OUGHT'

We can, incorrectly, see these three words as very positive. However, the opposite is true: every time we tell ourselves that we 'should' achieve top marks, or that we 'ought' to know the answer, or that we 'must' do better.

This isn't positive or balanced thinking at all. We are setting ourselves up for failure by suggesting that we are not good enough unless we achieve this or that. If we then don't achieve one of these 'should', 'must' or 'ought' tasks we set ourselves up for failure, and more negative beliefs about not being good enough, etc. will set in. While we believe that we are motivating ourselves, we are actually berating ourselves. For example, 'I must always be polite/charming/clever/etc., and if I am not then I'm worthless/boring/dreary/unlikeable/etc.

We often use these words when we describe aspects of others as well – how people 'should' care about something, how someone 'ought' to be more responsible, etc. It is a bad habit to get into and, in this case, it is very judgemental – just the thing we are trying to get away from. Others can behave how they like. It is nothing to do with us.

It will be far more helpful if you gathered up these three words, binned them and got into the habit of replacing them with softer alternatives, such as:

▶ 'It would be terrific to come top in the exam but if I don't, it's not the end of the world.'

▶ 'I would really like to get this work finished tonight but if I don't, I can come in early tomorrow.'

Soften it up, be less hard on yourself – and be more likely to succeed, as the pressure you are putting on yourself will be much less.

Try it now

Write down three sentences using 'should', 'must' or 'ought' in a way that relates to negative thoughts that you have/had about yourself in a recent situation. Then write the sentences again, having binned 'should', 'must' and 'ought'.

Observe others around you, or consider the behaviour of friends, family and colleagues. Ask yourself whether they also set themselves the harsh standards you set yourself? Consider:

▶ why they might be content with different views

▶ whether you personally judge them negatively for these more relaxed views

▶ whether you consider that others judge them negatively for these different views, these more relaxed ways of being?

What might this suggest to you about the way you look at things?

FINDING EVIDENCE

As with balanced thinking, gathering evidence to support a belief is a very helpful tool. You can do this using a positive data log. It is a simple but effective record encouraging you to note your negative beliefs and then look for evidence that might show that a belief isn't true *all the time*.

You are also encouraged to rate the strength of your belief and to review this rating on a regular basis as you continue to practise, so that you can note any, hopefully positive, changes.

This is what a positive data log might look like.

Self-critical belief: I am a selfish person.
How strongly I believe this: 80%

Alternative, more helpful belief: I am no more selfish than many people.
How strongly I believe this: 20%

Evidence to support my new belief and weaken my old belief:

I was thanked for my kindness by someone in the supermarket.

Although not naturally over-compassionate I work on empathizing with others.

What to me seems selfish – not calling my mother every day, for example – may seem quite normal to others.

In the scale of things, really selfish people are those who rob and harm others deliberately. I would never do that.

I notice that others can be selfish at times as well but I accept their good points and like them anyway.

Just acknowledging a trait is a good first step to reducing it.

Give a rating for how much you now believe your old belief (1%–100%) and your new belief (1%–100%). Check your belief rating on, say, a weekly basis and look for a reduction in the old belief rating and an increase in the new one.

Don't expect to reach 100 per cent. You are just training your mind to become more open to the possibility that you are being unrealistically hard on yourself (or others) and that a softer and more balanced view helps you to feel mentally and emotionally better. An 'on balance' view will be a good result and enable you to view situations in a more realistic way than previously.

Key idea

Be patient as you work for change. Don't be disappointed if change is slow and give up because of this. Even the slightest improvement is a success.

Remember this

We simply assume that the way we see things is the way they really are or the way they should be: and our attitudes and behaviours grow out of these assumptions.

Stephen Covey, *Everyday Greatness* (2006)

Focus points

* We have looked for the first time at the deeper layers of negative thinking that can cause us to maintain a pessimistic outlook. Hopefully you now appreciate the underpinning of beliefs and assumptions that come from early formative experiences which we carry forward with us and never test out or question.

* The skills we have suggested in this chapter are all helpful, but you may find that some suit you better than others. Test them out, and base your plan on using those that suit you best.

* As well as new techniques for reshaping unhelpful beliefs, you have discovered that many of the skills you have been using to challenge your NATs can also be adjusted slightly to challenge assumptions and beliefs.

* Remember, you may not need to work on faulty beliefs, which is why these aspects are introduced to you only now. If you find that adjusting your day-to-day thinking and behaviours makes a real difference to you, you don't need to look more deeply. If, however, you have found it all hard going, do ensure that you work hard on this chapter to see if this is where the problem lies.

Rate your effort (1–10) for the exercises you have tried in this chapter ......

Next step

Chapter 10 is something of a miscellany. In it, you will learn of several additional CBT techniques that can be used in conjunction with what you have learned so far and which will slot in where you need them. They are all useful and easy to learn and will add immensely to your toolbox of skills and techniques.

Adding to your toolbox

By the end of this chapter you should:

▶ *have a number of new skills and techniques to add to your toolbox*

▶ *understand these new 'tools' and be able to select those that seem especially helpful to you*

▶ *ensure these tools are put into safe keeping for future use.*

Self-assessment

1 Do your emotions leave you feeling exhausted?

2 Are you an empathetic friend when those you care about have difficulties, trying to help them see things in a more optimistic way and/or find solutions?

3 What do you understand by the term 'open questioning'?

4 Do you use open questioning when talking to a friend in difficulties?

5 Do you tend to think in pictures or in words? For example, if you are considering trying something new and difficult, how do you think about it?

I imagine your reaction to the above questions may be 'what a disparate load of unconnected enquiries'. In fact, they describe this chapter well as we are looking at a miscellany of additional CBT skills that you may find useful. If you have answered 'yes' to questions 1, 2, 4 and 5, you will find skills in this chapter that will help you to put the abilities you have recognized above to good use. If you are uncertain about the answer to question 3, you will learn about open questioning in this chapter. If you feel that you are well aware of what it is, you can build on this knowledge to develop it as a powerful tool to help you make your thinking more positive.

Building up your toolbox

So far, we have gradually built up a number of CBT skills through focusing on particular parts of the whole – looking at thoughts (including assumptions and beliefs), feelings and behaviours separately, so that you become familiar with them and have a full understanding of each component and how to work on changing their negative aspects to more balanced and optimistic ones. You will already have seen that many of the skills for change overlap. Some are specific, while others have very general uses. The skills in this chapter have very general applications. I like to think of this as having a metaphorical toolbox into which you can delve when you need some help and find a 'tool' that will be right for the job. So do add the skills described in this chapter to your own 'toolbox'. You will find them very helpful.

Becoming more curious

We are usually far more curious about other people's thoughts and feelings than we are about our own. We may feel 'down' or anxious but rarely ask ourselves about the detail of why we feel that way. Yet if a friend tells us the same thing we become excellent enquirers! We want to help them and have a genuine curiosity. We may ask them questions such as the following.

▶ 'What has happened to make you feel like this?'

▶ 'How long has this been going on for?'

▶ 'Have you thought of any solutions?'

▶ 'Could you consider…?'

We ask our friend helpful questions: questions that encourage them to look more specifically at the problem and to find a way forward, either through looking at things differently or through acting differently, which might help them feel better.

Our helpful questions are open, i.e. they require an answer that is thoughtful and considered rather than just a 'Yes/No' answer. They get our friend thinking. Yet we very rarely have these types of conversations with ourselves.

Remember this

This type of open questioning, aimed at guided discovery towards solutions for problems, is called Socratic enquiry after the Greek philosopher Socrates, who lived in Athens in 400 BC. He was famed for his questioning enquiry, which encouraged his students to reach conclusions about their concerns without his directly instructing them. This method works just as well today.

Developing an enquiring mind

Perhaps it seems a little odd to have such a conversation with ourselves. Yet think of all the other 'conversations' that are going on endlessly in our heads. Our 'chatterbox' rarely stops but we scarcely notice it. We need to make an appointment with ourselves and use empathetic, open questions to help ourselves to understand and resolve our own emotional or practical difficulties.

This method of enquiry forms the cornerstone of professional therapy, and there is no reason why you should not have open conversations with yourself, either in your head, or, if you have time, noting things down, which will have a stronger effect.

WHY IT IS SO POWERFUL

When your mood is low or you are worrying about something, your focus narrows to negative thoughts and beliefs that you consider to be the facts of the matter. Open questioning encourages you to look more broadly at your thinking and to stretch your mind to embrace concepts that might presently be buried deep and not within your current awareness. You may be missing some positive aspects of the situation or dismissing them as 'not counting'. You get a chance to reconsider, to offer yourself a wider selection of possibilities. Because you are asking questions rather than making statements, you give yourself a chance to re-evaluate your views and perhaps draw different conclusions.

ENQUIRING SELF-TALK

I am often asked 'What is a good question? Where can I find some good questions as I find it hard to come up with anything?'.

Try it now

Write down – and put what you have written somewhere that you can access easily when you need it – a variety of open questions that could apply to you generally or that you might ask someone else if you were helping them with a problem.

A few have already been mentioned, and I will give you two or three more to start you off. Don't stop until you get to around a dozen. These will be an excellent tool for your toolbox when you need them. Here are a few suggestions:

* Am I being unduly negative about what actually happened?
* Are there any other ways of looking at this?
* Have I any evidence to support my thoughts?
* How would I advise someone else who had to deal with this?

You are looking for answers that will encourage you to explore the situation further and possibly revise your current conceptualization (your map) of the problem.

Key idea

When working in this way you will move back and forth between concrete information (facts) and the abstract (your own views and interpretations). Ask yourself what you actually know to be a fact rather than a negative assumption you might be making, and then make an evaluation or look at your options with this increased knowledge.

OPEN QUESTIONING

Open questioning can change beliefs as well as thoughts. Usually we are less likely to question beliefs as they are exactly that – things that we believe to be absolutely true. Get into the habit of using open questioning to chip away at these beliefs. Is holding such a belief helpful? If not, why not? What evidence do I have that it is actually true? (Remember, facts only, please; not 'because I've always thought that it was'.) Do other people that you know believe the same thing? If not, why not? Who is right? What do you make of this?

There are many more good questions like these. All good questions will encourage you to ask yourself what your view is now about what worried you originally. Is your original belief still intact or are you less certain?

Key idea

It is important to appreciate that you are not trying to prove your thoughts and beliefs to be wrong. They may not be. The purpose is, especially if you are suffering emotionally, to check out all the evidence and options in the broadest way and then to review the validity of your initial thinking. It is 'guided discovery' rather than an attempt to prove a point.

KEEPING REMINDERS

Some people find that when they are especially distressed, emotions run high and their brain takes a holiday. When you are new to practising these skills it can be especially hard to recall in the heat of the moment exactly what the skills are and how it use them. Thoughts that came clearly and easily in the comfort of your home or in a quiet moment can desert you totally when negative emotions overwhelm you, or your mood is so low that your brain feels like cotton wool.

Written reminders can be extremely helpful at such times. Try to carry these around with you on, say, a small piece of card or in a file on your mobile phone or another electronic device.

First, think about when you are most likely to find it hard to get your brain into gear – if you suffer from panic attacks in lifts, for example, then lifts are going to be the place that rational thinking completely deserts you. Think ahead of time what your most common thoughts and feelings are in this situation and note these down. Then note down a strong, balanced rebuttal to your negative thought. Write down two or three options if you can.

Keep these reminders with you, and the next time your negative emotions overwhelm your rational thinking, get out an appropriate reminder and read the more positive, encouraging alternative that you have written on the other side. This will help you to become calmer and more balanced than you might have done without a prompt.

Using your imagination

This technique is often used on business courses where organizational staff are encouraged to picture themselves, say, successfully closing a deal. Top sportsmen work with sports psychologists to create images of themselves doing well in their sport, even picturing themselves being presented with the winner's trophy. Basically, they are picturing success before it actually happens to make it more likely that success will happen.

If working with visual imagery is of interest to you, do explore the expertise that is available to you to learn more about this particular tool.

Acting it out

This is something that you are less likely to do unless you are working with a professional, but do consider it – perhaps with a friend or anyone willing to help you. You are basically going to act out a feared situation but in a safe place with an empathetic helper acting along with you. An example of when this might be useful is if you are very nervous about some sort of confrontation with someone you feel will be stronger than you. Let's say you need to get a work colleague to change their mind about an important decision and the mere thought of discussing this leaves you weak at the knees. Ask your helper to play your work colleague (give them an idea of how you are expecting him/her to react so that they can get into the role) and you play yourself. Think about how you would like to be, what you would like to say, how you would like things to work out. Try it out. See how it goes. The chances are it will go well and give you lots of confidence for the real thing. You can also practise role reversal. You play the difficult colleague and ask your helper to be you. See how this works out and whether they think of things to say and do that you hadn't thought of. It will be helpful and the goal is to give you more confidence ahead of the actual situation.

Ask a friend

We have touched already on the technique of conducting a survey to discover how others view or deal with difficulties you find it hard to cope with, or ideas that you cannot dismiss or which you believe to be indisputable facts.

You can do this in a very informal way – your friends won't see you in a research role but just as an enquiring friend. Ask some colleagues in the office or a few friends in the coffee shop after aerobics:

▶ 'What is their view on…?'

▶ 'Do they worry about…?'

▶ 'How would they deal with…'.

This can be extremely enlightening. I have worked with clients who have been amazed to discover that their friends don't check at least three times that they've locked the back door or spend all day worrying that they might have cancer. It can be a revelation – and also food for thought, as it weakens the strength of the individual's belief that they need to think/behave this way themselves. Once you learn that others don't do this, you realize that perhaps you don't need to do it either. It is another confidence booster.

For example, if you worry that you stutter when you get nervous and that people will notice this and judge you adversely, try it out. Ask directions of someone in the street and stutter slightly as you speak. Do this quite often (it does take courage but it is worth it) and review the outcome. Who seemed to notice? Who seemed bothered? How did that affect how they dealt with you? What do you conclude from all this?

Our harshest taskmaster

We are always harder on ourselves than others. We rarely make allowances for ourselves as we would for our friends. We expect ourselves to get everything right and beat ourselves up for being no more than fallible human beings. The art of learning to be kinder to yourself can be developed by thinking about what you would say to a friend who was feeling about themselves as you do now. What would you say to them? Would you be sharp and critical and point out their weakness, or would you be encouraging and empathetic and help them see things in a more positive and balanced way? Almost certainly the latter.

Isn't it strange how much easier we find it to be constructive and positive with others? Equally, think about how your friends might respond to you if you opened up to them with regard to your anxieties or negative feelings. How would they respond to you? Are they likely to be cold and unsympathetic, or warm and encouraging?

Make a start at being your own best friend. Take the time to ask yourself:

▶ 'What would I say to Jane if she told me this?'

▶ 'What would John tell me if I explained my anxiety to him?'.

The answer you come up with will usually be quite different to your own negative thinking and will tell you a lot.

Try it now

Pick three negative aspects of yourself, or occasions when you felt you acted negatively, and ask yourself 'If a friend described themselves to me in this way, what would I tell them?'. Write your answers down to ensure that you give this proper thought rather than a mental 'rush through'. Does this give you a new perspective on your views about yourself?

As already mentioned, none of this is about proving that all negative thoughts are incorrect. Often they are not, and we do find ourselves behaving poorly, making negative predictions that turn out to be true or finding that things have gone terribly wrong. On occasions like these, coming up with a more optimistic angle on the problem – 'At least nobody died' or 'Thank goodness it wasn't a *total* disaster' – can help, but it doesn't necessarily enable you to cope with the difficult situation you find yourself in.

Develop a disaster relief plan

When worrying about a problem, ask yourself:

▶ 'What is the worst-case scenario I could predict'

▶ 'If it happened, how would I manage?'

This type of question will help you develop your coping skills. We have within us all the resources we need to help us in difficult circumstances, but until they are called upon it is hard to appreciate that they will appear. I have always loved a phrase in Ernest Hemingway's *For Whom the Bell Tolls*: 'Cometh the hour, cometh the man.' This is about you. You have everything you need within you to deal with crises, difficult circumstances or negative events.

To bring these resources to life you need to ask yourself the question, 'How will I cope if the worst possible scenario isn't down to my negative viewpoint but becomes a reality?'.

This question invites you to start to develop a coping mechanism. When I ask my clients this question, they often answer that they have no idea as they have never thought about it. They are too wrapped up in thoughts and emotions that lead them to think in terms of 'It would be unbearable' or 'It doesn't bear thinking about', and no one takes themselves beyond that, into the realms of what they would actually do.

You are asking yourself a very practical question, so give yourself a practical answer. Become action-oriented. Think about what you could do, if anything, to make things better. Ask yourself how you would cope if the worst comes to the worst.

This removes your negative belief 'I won't be able to cope' and replaces it with a question 'How will I cope?'. This might present a completely new way of looking at the problem that you haven't considered before.

You will derive great confidence from this. Think constantly in solution-focused mode, rather than trying to see things differently. Becoming active will help you cope better emotionally with a difficult problem.

Deconstructive and constructive thinking

The US psychologist Christine Padesky describes these two ways of thinking as very helpful in achieving good outcomes in CBT, and I think you will also find them helpful.

Use *deconstructive* thinking to 'desconstruct' a vague negative overview of something so that you have smaller, more specific component parts to work on. For example, instead of making a general statement such as 'I'm so stressed; I never have enough time', break it down into specifics:

▶ What are you stressed about (exactly, not vaguely)?

▶ What takes up your time?

▶ How would having more time help you?

Questions like this will help you to formulate exactly what is happening rather than leaving you with a vague overview that sounds distressing but without any particular direction to it.

Constructive thinking will then help you to look at the difficulty in a way that might begin to develop a solution. Ask questions such as:

▶ 'Can I change this?'

▶ 'If so, how can I change this?

▶ What should I be looking at/thinking about/doing?'

▶ 'Who might help me?'

▶ 'Are there any good aspects to this?'.

This type of questioning will help you to develop solutions to the problem rather than continue to ruminate on how stressed you are and how little time there is. Thus, you are constructing a new way of dealing with something that is more helpful to you.

Becoming mindful

Mindfulness is a wonderful skill for calming you and keeping you grounded. There is a chapter on mindfulness later in the book that I encourage you to read carefully and then research further; take a course if you can. In its simplest form, you are looking at the idea of what we call cognitive bias. That is, we lean towards a certain way of looking at things depending on our mood. We might be so busy focusing on a negative thinking bias that we fail to be mindfully aware of the present moment, of what is around us – of the coffee we have just drunk or the trees we have just walked among. Bringing yourself into awareness of your surroundings, both visually and through listening, will diminish your negative thinking and refocus your mind on the calm of the moment.

Exercise – the natural anti-depressant

You might not expect to find a psychological textbook discussing physical therapy, but there is a strong mind-body connection here that it may help you to be aware of.

If you find yourself visiting the doctor because of low mood, he/she might offer you the option of anti-depressant medication. Are you aware that you can manufacture your own? When you undertake reasonably strenuous physical exercise, your brain manufactures its own serotonin. This is the chemical that your doctor will be giving you in tablet form. So don't miss this free opportunity to improve your mood.

Try it now

Cover the page below and make a written note of what you consider the benefits of exercise to be. How many can you come up with?

Here are some possibilities. Exercise decreases your blood pressure, lowers your heart rate, slows your breathing, keeps essential muscle groups in good shape and keeps your weight down, which in turn helps prevent diseases of obesity, such as diabetes, stroke, etc. Exercise keeps energy levels up, oxygenates your body (keeping your blood and circulation healthy), and reduces stress via all of the above and also by rechannelling your energy into something constructive for your well-being.

How many of these benefits did you identify? Taken altogether, exercise is one of the greatest mood-lifters around. Don't ignore it.

Never give up

This may sound a rather hackneyed and obvious tip, but one of the main reasons that people don't change – or not as much as they would like to – is that they give up on the hard work and effort required to make positive changes. For example, you may be hoping that a quick glance through a self-help book will give you many new insights that you can easily put into practice. However, you find that this is not the case and then the questions is more difficult – 'How much work and effort am I prepared to put in to achieve the changes I want?'. Only you know the answer to that but I will mention that one of the reasons CBT is so popular is that it does have a high success rate for people who persevere with its techniques. Some find it life-changing. So it really is worth the effort. Don't say 'It's too hard' or 'I don't have time' or 'It doesn't make sense' or 'It doesn't work'. These expressions mean that you haven't been trying hard enough for long enough. In order to *really* know something, it must become part of your thinking, your emotions, your actions and reactions. This is about taking responsibility for your development.

Remember this

Dr Robert Anthony cites research (1979) that shows it takes approximately 21 days of daily practice to break an old, destructive habit or form a new, positive habit. Please keep this in mind.

Try it now

In the past year, what have you given up, and why? Write these things down and think about each one in turn for a moment. There will be good and valid reasons for some, but not for all. When have you used any of the negative thought ideas we have suggested above? Do you have any regrets about some of the things you gave up? What do you learn from this?

Focus points

✳ 'Horses for courses' means different things for different occasions, and CBT is excellent at providing a wide variety of skills and techniques to help different circumstances and individual preferences.

✳ Develop a 'toolbox' of skills that work for you: skills that you understand, have practised and feel confident in. Always search for something to help you – if one doesn't work, perhaps another will.

✳ Of particular significance is the idea that many of you will find it easier to think in terms of images rather than words, and it is important that you have a set of tools that is especially helpful with this way of visualizing events and situations. We have only touched briefly on this area here but if you are a visual person, do explore these skills in more depth.

✻ Open questioning means having a conversation with yourself that is as empathetic, as curious, as thoughtful and as constructive as those you might have with other people. Never give yourself, or accept from others you might be trying to help, a Yes/No answer unless it is especially appropriate.

✻ Don't give up. While not technically a CBT skill, it is vital to success, and you may require encouragement to keep practising some new ideas which seem hard and/or where positive results are not immediately forthcoming.

✻ Exercise!

Rate your effort (1–10) for the exercises you have tried in this chapter ......

Next step

Chapter 11 looks at symptom relief, and whether any is appropriate. CBT isn't intended to provide you with tips for calming you down when you have a panic attack or helping you to live with depression. Its premise is that it wants to cure you of panic attacks, depressive episodes, etc., not to help you to live with them. So CBT therapists don't focus on relieving the symptoms but on complete cure. However, there are some circumstances where it would be little short of cruel not to give a helping hand to those who are working hard at overcoming their problems but still experiencing harsh symptoms: as if we were insisting that you climb Everest without oxygen.

So in Chapter 11 we look at the different forms of symptom relief, weigh up their pros and cons, and ask you to make informed decisions about them.

Symptom relief

By the end of this chapter you will be:

▶ *more aware of the pros and cons of symptom relief*

▶ *able to decide when symptom relief merely maintains a problem (or even makes it worse) and when it may be helpful.*

Self-assessment

1 When you feel physically anxious or stressed, how do you relieve these feelings?

2 Does what you do resolve your problems?

3 Permanently?

4 If not, why not?

5 Do the answers to questions 2, 3 and 4 make you look at your symptom relief techniques differently?

The point of these questions is to find out what reliance you may have at present on symptom relief. Symptom relief is any action that prevents you from feeling physically horrible because of worries or low mood. A good example would be avoiding going to an event you were anxious about. What a relief when you decide not to go! However, the answers you give to these questions should also get you thinking about how helpful symptom relief really is. If you now have any doubts about it as a tool, this chapter will be helpful to you.

Errors masquerading as solutions

One of the advantages of professional therapy is that the therapist is there to guide you from the wrong path back on to the right one. If you are acting as your own therapist and guide, it is important for you to understand the wrong turnings you can unintentionally take and to do what you can to avoid these, or correct them if you have already started off down the wrong path.

We have already discussed how one danger of symptom relief is that it can masquerade as a solution to the problem. In fact, it is a solution only to how you *feel* about the problem – and even if for a short period of time you do feel better, the symptom relief doesn't resolve the problem itself, which will still be there.

So always use symptom relief in an informed and occasional way, at the same time appreciating that it can become a behavioural error if you try to use it as an alternative to addressing your problems.

Later in this chapter we will explore the types of symptom relief which it might be worth using on an occasional basis. First, however, let's address some symptom relief errors, both of thought and action, that may trip you up and leave you frustrated and in a hole.

Key idea

Look at thinking and behavioural errors as 'maintaining behaviours'. Although we may *think* we are finding a solution by relieving our symptom(s), we are actually doing things that, at their very best, maintain and cement the problem; for example, how does always taking the stairs help you to get over your lift phobia?. At its worst, maintaining behaviours cement a problem so that it becomes even harder to dislodge. A good question to ask yourself, as you pull the duvet over your head or decline a stressful engagement, is: 'Is doing this going to help me *feel* better, or actually *get* better?' There is a huge difference, which I hope you are now able to appreciate.

Beware the perils of symptom relief in maintaining rather than removing problems. Here are some more symptom relief errors.

THE 'IT'S ALL TOO MUCH' ERROR

Low mood and depression can leave us feeling physically exhausted. I have yet to meet a depressed person who did not feel tired all the time and saw the, seemingly obvious, solution to this as constant rest: not even getting out of bed in cases of severe depression. 'Hiding under the duvet' is the common way of describing how we may react to feeling down. The thought is – again, seemingly sensibly – that once we have rested and feel more energized, we will get on and face the world.

What we actually find is that making any sort of effort is, well, an effort. A big effort. So perhaps we'll just sit a little longer, go back to bed, call in sick, cancel that social engagement, just until we feel more like it.

However, this leaves you trapped in a maintaining behaviour. The less you do, the less you want to do. If you stay home instead of going out you lose your social skills, so the thought of going out becomes even more horrendous. Friends start to wonder where you are, and then stop wondering and forget you, which can trigger all sorts of 'Nobody cares about me' negative automatic thoughts (NATs). Not trying new things does save you from possible failure but you never feel the positive emotions of success. Being sedentary instead of taking exercise will make you feel physically worse. In turn, this encourages you to believe that you need to rest even more. Your motivation disappears and you are in a vicious circle of maintaining your low mood. Ring any bells? If you feel this may apply to you, Chapter 13 on overcoming depression will give you the skills to break out of this cycle. As you will discover, the answer to this particular error lies in beginning to adopt a 'do the opposite' approach in order to get better.

Clients sometimes say to me, 'Once I feel more confident, then I will do more'. Unfortunately, it is the other way around; it is doing more that gives you more confidence.

> ### Remember this
> Mistakes are a part of being human. Appreciate your mistakes for what they are: precious life lessons that can only be learned the hard way – unless it's a fatal mistake, which, at least, others can learn from.
> Alan Franken, US political commentator

THE 'WATCHFUL' ERROR
Imagine that you have a friend who has been seriously ill or a family member who has died of cancer or heart failure This might trigger thoughts along the lines of 'Suppose this were to happen to me?'. Although that would not be unnatural, what *is* unnatural is for you to decide that the only way to prevent this is to become hyper-vigilant and be constantly alert to, and act on, any unusual aches, pains or twinges. This seems like an excellent idea – you certainly don't want to miss an early indication that your fears may be about to materialize.

Answer this

Now you understand more about symptom relief errors, what error do you think is being made here? Can you work it out?

Hopefully, you will have been able to work out the error. Indeed, the problem with focusing so strongly on your symptoms in this way is that you will have a negative bias towards finding evidence to support your worries. A slight twinge in your arm will need to be investigated rather than left to go away of its own accord. What could it mean? You will feel too anxious not to get it checked out. This might involve visits to the doctor, searching the internet (where you discover a whole raft of extra fatal possibilities) or asking your friends and family what they think about it.

Does this reduce your worries? On the contrary, you will have increased them. To learn more about overcoming this thinking and behavioural error, read Chapters 14 and 15 on anxiety.

THE 'NARROW FOCUS' ERROR

Imagine someone asking you to go out into the garden and count how many sparrows you saw sitting in the trees. Most people discover when they focus on something in this way, that there are either more or less of the items than they thought. They are focusing on the head count and also evaluating it. Natural logic.

However, if, when you came back indoors with this information, the person then asked you how many thrushes you had seen, what would you say? You might be able to tell them exactly how many thrushes there were. The more likely answer, however, would be that you didn't know – because you weren't focusing on thrushes, just sparrows.

This is called *selective focus,* and we do it all the time without realizing it. We may think that we are absorbing what is around us in an equal and level way but this is rare. It usually depends on our thinking at that time. If you are worried about growing old, you are likely to notice just how many people there are with walking sticks and Zimmer frames. If you long for a baby, pregnant mothers are everywhere.

Now imagine that you have concerns about yourself. For example, perhaps you consider that you are a poor conversationalist and bore people. If so, your focus is more likely to be on the behaviour of others that supports this view rather than on behaviour that discounts it. If someone looks away when talking to you, you are more likely to interpret that as a slight than as an innocuous mannerism. If someone introduces you to their friend, you may assume that they are tired of you themselves and are trying to 'palm you off'. This negative focus will prevent you from noticing someone else smiling at you, or recalling the plate of nibbles offered to you by a friend earlier on. Your focus is selective and negatively biased – and as such, it maintains your problem.

THE 'I'LL DO IT LATER' ERROR

'Never do today what you can put off until tomorrow' is a common phrase that inverts a well-known proverb and makes us smile. However, procrastination is another term for avoidance. It involves putting off things that we should be facing and dealing with. What you are doing is finding excuse after excuse not to tackle something that might be difficult, even when this might make things a lot better: asking the boss for the pay rise you are due; discussing with your partner how you can more fairly share the chores; telling your parents that you don't want to go to them for Christmas this year. All things that we can easily put off, but how does this resolve the problem?

'I'll sort it out in a few weeks' time.' 'I'll get a job soon.' 'I'll wait and see what happens – maybe things will change.' The problem with procrastination is that it is disempowering. The more you shy away from dealing with difficult things the harder they become to face and you lose the ability to act on something that would have a positive effect on your life.

THE 'I'LL JUST GO OVER IT AGAIN IN MY MIND' ERROR

When we ruminate, we return to past negative events (or events that seem distressing now, with the benefit of hindsight) and we turn them over in our minds again and again without adding anything new or optimistic that might cause us to look at the events differently. 'If only I hadn't done that', 'If only I had realized', 'Why did things have to turn out that way?'. We go over and over the same old ground, becoming sadder and more depressed as we do so.

This is understandable, of course; it is often difficult to put past upsets and disappointments behind us. This isn't to say that we should not look back at past upsets, but we need to do so with insight, seeking to find new ways to deal with things that are helpful to us, not simply regurgitating them. A good question to ask yourself if you do find yourself locked into negative ruminations are: 'What have I learned from this experience that can make me stronger now?'. This helps you to break the negative cycle and try to find something positive from your past disappointments.

Try it now

Identify any thinking or behavioural errors described above that you might make, either occasionally or regularly. Now think of an action plan to eliminate these errors or replace them with more helpful thoughts and actions.

For example, if you realize that inactivity is a problem for you, make a weekly activity schedule to ensure that you are keeping busy and active. If you spend time on the internet researching possible reasons for that twinge in your arm, ban yourself from doing so. Try this new regime for a week and then reflect and observe changes in your thoughts and your moods as a result of it. Make similar action plans for any of the other errors that you think might apply to you.

Using symptom relief to reduce physical stress

There is a place for the relief that reduces physical symptoms but this should be used wisely and in the understanding that you are not resolving your problems but simply providing a temporary replenishing of your body in order to be better able to cope with finding a proper solution.

Our emotions have a strong effect on our bodies. Chronic low mood can be as physically exhausting as running a half-marathon. Feeling anxious or panicky can cause our heart to race, our stomach to churn and our muscles to tense – all wearing and unpleasant effects. In some cases, people fear that they may be seriously ill and take themselves to the doctor or the hospital.

Sleep can be a problem. Lack of sleep in turn causes exhaustion, which compounds our physiological symptoms and makes everything even worse.

Because feeling this way physically is so wretched, most people, even when told that they are physically fine, want to find a way to stop feeling like this. They look for relief from the physical symptoms.

The problem with symptom relief for problems that are emotional rather than physical is that, while you may temporarily feel better, it hasn't dealt with the root cause, i.e. whatever is causing your negative, anxious thoughts. So modern therapy tends to dismiss symptom relief as a 'sticking plaster effect' and not helpful to lasting solutions.

However, this is not an absolute view. It depends very much on whether the individual has access to professional help or enough knowledge to help themselves using CBT techniques. I work with some people who are so distressed that asking them to 'stick with it' and undertake challenges of any sort is beyond them. They need to feel a little better first.

Key idea

As long as you understand symptom relief is not the solution to your difficulties but simply something to make life more bearable for a short while until you work out what to do, use it if you need to.

If you fall into the category I have mentioned above – you do not have professional help and have, as yet, to master the CBT techniques that will help you – use the following on a temporary basis. But do remember that this is just a temporary respite until you resolve your problems – it is not the solution to them.

DISTRACTION

Distraction can be helpful as we are not able to think of two things at once. If you are thinking about a work meeting tomorrow, you will not also be deciding what to watch on TV tonight. If you are adding up in your head how much money you have spent this week, you cannot also be compiling the shopping list. The idea is, therefore, that focusing on relaxing, pleasant thoughts may prevent our negative worries dominating us.

However, many people find it difficult to learn the ability to free themselves from their worrying thoughts. The more they try to dismiss their worries, the more they won't go away. The simple principal of 'That which we resist, persists' gets in the way. If I offered you a lot of money not to think about pink elephants for five minutes I would win the bet – you would be able to think of nothing else. Equally, if I offered you a lot of money to tell me if you had (truthfully!) thought of pink elephants before I mentioned them, you almost certainly would not have. It is the act of attempting to block a thought that makes it come into our minds and stay there.

So don't even attempt to get rid of your negative thoughts.

Replace them instead.

With what sort of thing?

The type of distraction that works best is different for everyone, but you need to have a few things that are easily accessible up your sleeve.

Try it now

Note down a few things that you find quite absorbing and interesting. For some, it might be reading a book or doing a Sudoku puzzle. For others, it might be talking to a friend about holidays or watching a particular programme on TV. Perhaps going for a walk or a run, working out in the gym.

Or if you are away from home with nothing around you, simply counting birds on the telegraph wires or white cars in the street will be effective.

Now, when your negative thoughts creep in and leave you feeling physically distressed, pick any one thing and distract yourself with it. Don't try to eliminate your negative thoughts; just focus on whatever it is you have chosen to do.

Note how you feel after 5, 10 and 15 minutes. Are you calmer? Is your body a little more relaxed? If so, you have learned a new skill. Distraction. Very useful on occasions.

THE BENEFITS OF BREATHING

There is a therapeutic view that breathing and relaxation techniques are forms of symptom relief to be avoided. However, there are different views about this, and many factors need to be taken into account before rejecting these out of hand I personally believe that good breathing is extremely helpful as it is what we should all be doing anyway. So learning it via a CBT self-help book is as good a way as any to get you on track to improving something so vital to your well-being.

 Try it now

What is the purpose of breathing? On the face of it, this sounds a ridiculous question. The answer, surely, is 'To stay alive.' Isn't it? Well, yes, but why else is breathing good for us? Stop and think for a moment. Write down any other reasons that breathing might be helpful if you can think of them. Then compare what you have written with the list below.

First, breathing helps to carry oxygen round our body. I tend to think of the analogy of a little grocer's van delivering oxygen to our bloodstream. The bloodstream in turn acts like a grocery store, moving round the body and providing its various parts with the amounts of the things that they need to keep healthy.

Secondly, good breathing ensures that oxygen gets to our brains to help us think faster, better and at a higher level.

Thirdly, it helps to keep our heart rate and blood pressure down.

You may have studied yoga (if not, consider it) and know that the 'calming breath' suggests that breathing is good for your soul as well as your body. A good supply of oxygen also deprives cancer cells of the conditions they need to flourish and, most importantly for the purposes of managing emotion, breathing helps you to relax.

Did you get all of these? If not, don't worry. I usually forget it all until a reminder makes me refocus on the many important reasons for breathing well.

Much has been written and taught about good breathing. You may already follow instructions that are similar to the suggestions below or you may have a different way of practising, which you should stick to if you find it helpful. However, you may not, up to now, have paid much attention to breathing and if you have not, do spend some time trying out these techniques as they have so many benefits.

Try it now

Many experts suggest that you count your breaths in and out, but this can cause some people to hyperventilate or to concentrate too much on counting and not on breathing. So unless you find counting helpful, simply find a rhythm that is comfortable and breathing that is slow and deep.

Although you can do this exercise while lying down, bear in mind that the goal is for you to be able use this skill 'whenever and wherever', so sitting, or even standing, will be a better option.

* Breathe in through your nose and out through your mouth. You can try making each exhalation a little longer than each inhalation.
* Ensure that you breathe from your diaphragm and not from your chest.
* Relax your shoulders and upper chest muscles when you breathe, and keep working on this until you feel naturally more relaxed.

Key idea

If you wish to use breathing techniques as symptom relief when you start to feel anxious or panicky, you need to practise it regularly, several times a day. Don't wait for a crisis to use this skill as you will be flustered already so trying to recall a breathing skill when you are in panic mode will be impossible.

Try it now

Take time to become aware of your breathing when you are:
* in a stressful situation
* relaxing.
Notice whether your breathing gets deeper or shallower, faster or slower. At what time of the day is your breathing at its absolute slowest?

MUSCLE RELAXATION

The idea behind practising muscular relaxation is that it will eventually enable you to relax yourself quickly and at will, thus helping you to reduce strong emotions before they become out of control. As with the breathing exercises, you need to practise initially on a daily basis so that you have a good grasp of the skill before you are in a crisis and your emotional brain is flooding out your rational brain.

Progressive muscle relaxation follows this process:

▶ tense a group of muscles so that they are as tightly contracted as possible

▶ hold the muscles in a state of extreme tension for a few seconds (it may be helpful to count to 10)

▶ then relax the muscles to their previous state

▶ keep the muscles in this relaxed state for around 20 seconds, and then start to tense them again.

Tensing your muscles first will help you to relax your muscles more subsequently than would be the case if you tried to relax your muscles directly. I suggest you try all of the exercises suggested below and then pick out a few that work well for you. Eventually reduce these further to just one or two exercises that you can 'carry around' with you for use anywhere.

Try it now

* Hands – form a fist, clenching your hand as tightly as you can. Then relax your hand to its previous tension, and then consciously relax it again so that it is as loose as possible. You should feel deep relaxation in your hand muscles. You might also say to yourself 'relax' as you do so.
* Arms – bend an elbow and tense all the muscles in the arm for a few seconds as you breathe in. Then relax as you breathe out. Repeat with the other arm.
* Neck – press your head back as hard as is comfortable and roll it slowly from side to side. Then relax.
* Face – try to frown and lower your eyebrows as hard as you can for a few seconds. Then relax. Then raise your eyebrows (as if you were startled) as hard as you can, then relax. Then clench your jaw for a few seconds, then relax.
* Chest – take a deep breath and hold it for a few seconds. Then relax and go back to normal breathing.
* Stomach – tense the stomach muscles as tight as possible. Then relax.
* Buttocks – squeeze the buttocks together as much as possible. Then relax.
* Legs – with your legs flat on the floor, bend your feet and toes towards your face as hard as you can, and then relax. Then bend your feet and toes away from your face for a few seconds, and then relax.

RELIEVING SLEEP DIFFICULTIES

I would also like to mention sleep difficulties as they are often experienced by people with depression or anxiety. When we are suffering from stress or low mood our sleep pattern can go haywire. We cannot sleep at all, sleep fitfully, wake several times in the night between small episodes of sleep or wake early in the morning and are unable to sleep further.

Not only does disrupted sleep or lack of sleep cause us to function below par, it increases our worries. We feel that if, on top of everything else, we cannot now rely on a good night's sleep then we have lost one last helpful haven of calm.

Sometimes, if we worry about not having had enough sleep our brain transmits this worry message to our body and we feel tired 'to order'. If we took less notice of the amount of sleep we have had (recall the 'negative focusing' error we discussed earlier), then we will probably feel less tired.

Reducing your worries about sleep is likely to lead to better sleep. There are several ways that you can do this.

▶ It is a fatal mistake to lie in the darkness 'trying everything' to get to sleep. You will never get to sleep by 'trying'. Accept that you are unable to sleep at the moment and enjoy simply lying in a warm and cosy environment. This will relax you, which in turn will help you to drift off to sleep. The moment you become anxious about not sleeping, you are consigning yourself to a wakeful night. You can only fall asleep when your body and brain is relaxed, so worrying about it makes sleep impossible.

▶ Have confidence in the research evidence that to lie resting is as good for our bodies as actually sleeping. It isn't as good as sleep for our minds, but our bodies will benefit enormously from being prone and resting. Knowing this will help you to relax further. You are doing the best for your body simply by being in bed and allowing it to rest.

▶ It can take about 20 minutes, on average, to fall asleep, even for heavy sleepers. So don't worry about lying awake. Just use the time to relax.

▶ Rather than worrying about not sleeping, use your CBT thought-challenging techniques to relax yourself. See the table below for examples.

Negative thought	Balanced alternative
I should be able to sleep well every night like a normal person. I shouldn't have a problem!	Lots of people struggle with sleep from time to time. I will be able to sleep with practice.
It's the same every single night, another night of sleepless misery.	Not every night is the same. Some nights I do sleep better than others.
If I don't get some sleep, I'll ruin my presentation and jeopardize my job.	I can get through the presentation even if I'm tired. I can still rest and relax tonight, even if I can't sleep.
I'm never going to be able to sleep well. It's out of my control.	Insomnia can be cured. If I stop worrying so much and focus on positive solutions, I can beat it.
It's going to take me at least an hour to get to sleep tonight. I just know it.	I don't know what will happen tonight. Maybe I'll get to sleep quickly if I use the strategies I've learned.

Remember this

The more trouble you have with sleep, the more it starts to invade your thoughts. You may dread going to sleep because you just know that you're going to toss and turn for hours or be up at 2 a.m. again. Or maybe you're worried because you have a big day tomorrow, and if you don't get a solid eight hours' sleep, you're sure you'll ruin it. But agonizing and expecting sleep difficulties only make insomnia worse. Worrying about getting to sleep or how tired you're going to be floods your body with adrenaline, and before you know it you're wide-awake.

Focus points

* While we have attempted to flag up thinking and behavioural errors that you might be making in each chapter of the book so far, there are a few more that you need to be aware of and we have included them in this chapter.
* Often, these errors come in the form of symptom relief that seems like a good thing, but which maintain or entrenches our problems rather than resolving them.
* It is important that you learn to spot these errors and be resilient in not using them, as they will hinder your progress.

* There are, however, some types of symptom relief that, provided you use them in an informed way can be of benefit. These are distraction, breathing and relaxation.
* Sleep can also become a problem when we are troubled so we have looked at ways to help you by regularizing your sleep pattern.
* These are all errors that can be easily adjusted, but you need first to recognize them and identify how they negatively impact on your life.

Rate your effort (1–10) for the exercises you have tried in this chapter ......

Next step

Much of what we have looked at, learned about and worked on so far has been focused on moving our mind away from its relentless 'chatterbox' of unproductive, negative thinking and we now have a variety of skills for achieving this and maintaining a more balanced, open-minded outlook. Running parallel with this is what has become known as mindful thinking. It is another way of enabling us to still our minds and bring our thoughts into the present moment, rather than trawling back over things or racing ahead to feel concern about things that haven't yet happened. Growing hugely in popularity owing to its researched and audited positive outcomes, mindfulness is not just a treatment protocol but a complete way of living. We look at it in Chapter 12.

Mindfulness

By the end of this chapter you will:

▶ *have gained a basic understanding of mindfulness and its process*

▶ *be able to decide whether to learn more by taking one of the many short mindfulness courses that are now available.*

Self-assessment

1 Have you ever sat in a talk or lecture and realized halfway through that you have followed very little of what has been said?

2 Do you eat your food quickly/glance quickly at the newspaper/cut short unproductive conversations, so that you can 'get on'?

3 Would you say that you regularly have too much to do and suffer from the mental stress of having several 'to do' lists in your head at once?

4 Do you pay particular attention to what is going on when you are performing day-to-day tasks or do you perform them robotically while thinking of other things?

5 Do you find it very easy to be judgemental, usually in a negative way?

How many of the above questions did you answer 'yes' to? Don't berate yourself for five 'yes' answers. This is normal. This is what most of us do, most of the time. But do we feel good about ourselves living this way? Rushing this way? Noticing little and enjoying even less?

There is another way. It is not an easy way (although it may sound it) and you would need to incorporate it into your daily life on a permanent basis. If you would consider this, you will be interested in 'mindfulness'.

It isn't possible to teach you the 'how to' of mindfulness in a book chapter, as, first, it is something that you need to try experientially, and secondly, it is a complex process that cannot be summed up in a few paragraphs and exercises. What I wish to do is to give you an understanding of mindfulness, in the hope this will encourage you to attend a course and really get some benefit from it.

Key idea

Mindfulness cannot be fully understood in a book chapter. Many practitioners would argue that it cannot be understood in a book. Mindfulness need to be *experienced*.

Why is mindfulness different?

Mindfulness is one of the oldest 'ways of being' (note that I am carefully not calling this a 'technique', for reasons I'll explain later). It has been translated into modern Western parlance and has gained enormous popularity, to the extent that it is now regularly used as a cure for depression.

Mindfulness is a form of meditation. It originally came from ancient Oriental teachings, but in the past 30 years has been especially developed by an American doctor, Jon Kabat-Zinn, who started a treatment programme that he called Mindfulness-based Stress Reduction at the University of Massachusetts Medical School. Initially intended to help those in chronic pain, it is now widely used to help a variety of problems, particularly depression. Mindfulness has been audited and evaluated and its results are impressive. A large proportion of those undertaking the programme remain depression-free in the long term, provided that they continue to practise what they have learned and build it into their lives.

In the 1990s, three eminent psychologists (Zindel Segal, Mark Williams and John Teasdale) visited Massachusetts to study Kabat-Zinn's programme and used it to develop a further use for mindfulness. They called this Mindfulness-based CBT.

Both of these therapeutic approaches have become hugely popular, many teachers have been trained and courses are widely available.

Key idea

I refer to mindfulness as a 'way of being' rather than a set of techniques. This is because you need to approach it in this way yourself. Mindfulness isn't a few skills that you can learn and bring out when you need them. It is a way of being that encourages you to adopt a whole new view of life that will bring you peace and contentment. To this extent, it is hard to master and you must consider it a life-long process – but one you will enjoy.

So far our premise has been the idea that if our thoughts and beliefs are unduly negative and cause us pain and despair, then working to validate (or invalidate) them – to see that pessimism and fear are not always founded on facts but on unhelpful negative assumptions that we can change – can be not only helpful but life-changing. Mindfulness offers a different way of feeling better those we have previously considered.

Mindfulness is essentially about awareness and the ability to 'enjoy the moment'. For most of us, our brains chatter on relentlessly, either trawling back through past events – going over a long list of 'If only's' and regrets, wishing things had been different, wondering how things might have been if they had, etc. – or looking ahead to the future and worrying and wondering, 'What if... this?', 'Supposing... that?', 'How will I... the other?'. On and on goes our brain, keeping us occupied with chat that seems to us like problem-solving but which is actually digging us deeper into the mire of being eternally depressed and anxious.

Have you ever done this? You make yourself a cup of tea or coffee, take it with you to your seat and take a sip. After a while you think you'll take another sip and pick up your cup – to find there is no coffee left in the cup. Without even noticing it, you have drunk the lot.

Or perhaps you've done this? You have to drive from A to B and you know the route well. You get into the driving seat and start off. As you drive, your head becomes a chatterbox of thoughts and concerns. Before you know it, here you are at place B. Can you recall anything about your journey at all? Did you see any squirrels, children playing, cars with new number plates, etc? No, of course not. You weren't paying attention to the present moment. You were living in your head, making your lists, going through how much you had to do before next Thursday, how to tell your wife that you had a crucial work presentation on school sports day, and so on.

There is nothing wrong with this. We all do it most of the time. But we are missing the present moment. In mindfulness terms, we are in 'doing mode' rather than 'being mode'.

DOING MODE

We are in doing mode when our brain is constantly trying to resolve a problem. This may be conscious, such as 'How will I find the time to complete my project?', or unconscious, such as walking from home to the park when the brain is working all the time to figure out what needs to be done – put one foot in front of other, walk this way, turn left there, get closer to end destination. Your brain is working on your behalf all the time. The brain's natural propensity is to look at two positions:

▶ Position A: where you are now

▶ Position B: where you would like/need to be.

This can be in terms of geography or in terms of work promotions, relationships or even just cooking the dinner. The brain's task is to help you to narrow the gap between A and B until B is achieved. This is the brain's 'doing mode'. Unfortunately, 'doing mode' can be tiring and stressful and doesn't always give us the solutions we want, which can make us feel more stressed and hopeless.

This is not to decry 'doing mode'. We need to be active and to be problem-solvers. But we also need to know when to switch off, i.e. when 'doing mode' becomes unhelpful and stops us enjoying life.

BEING MODE

In the words of Jon Kabat-Zinn, 'Mindfulness means paying attention in a particular way: on purpose, in the present moment and non-judgementally'. This is 'being mode'. It is the opposite of 'doing mode', which is driven, goal-oriented, relentlessly trying to reduce the gap between how things are and how we would like them to be. Whereas the focus of 'being mode' is on accepting and allowing things to be how they are without immediately going into a more pressured 'how do I change this?' way of thinking.

As with all things, there is a time and a place for each mode. Mindfulness is not about learning to put everything permanently to one side while you live your life accepting all

that is going on around you. It is about being able to find time
within your day, your week, your life, to relieve the stress,
to move away from low mood and to be calmly and non-
judgementally present in the moment, with awareness of your
experiences and calmly paying attention.

The benefits of mindfulness

What do we get from learning to be mindful? One answer
to this question is the slightly frustrating 'Whatever it means
to you'. Mindfulness is simply a way of being, and this is
individual to each of us. Practitioners even say that it cannot
be written about but only experienced. The emphasis on
experiential learning is because of this individual benefit. It is
what it is for you. You *will* get a great deal from it, but it will
take time and come only gradually, and how you personally feel
may be different from anyone else.

Key idea

The aim of mindfulness is not to teach you to relax, but to be aware.
As Jon Kabat-Zinn has said, 'Mindfulness is not about falling asleep. It is
about falling awake'. Don't worry if you find these concepts difficult at
first. When you start (if you do) to experience mindful practice, everything
will become clearer.

However, more concrete answers to the question of how
learning to be mindful benefits us would be the following.

▶ Increasing your awareness. Mindfulness will help you to
  notice in a positive way the sights and sounds around you.
  You will become more aware of everything you see, hear,
  smell. You will be aware of where you are, how you feel –
  and you will be in the present moment.

▶ Relaxing your body and getting back in touch with it
  through mindfulness meditation.

- Creating a calmer mind by taking a step back from your thoughts and ruminations (the main goal of most people who try mindfulness).

- Pain reducation. If you suffer from physical pain, mindfulness can help to reduce it. Many people who have 'tried everything' have found mindfulness to work when nothing else did.

- Standing away from your thoughts without blocking them. 'That which we resist, persists' so we cannot block out our thoughts, but we can learn to stand back and observe them without them swamping us. This enables us to evaluate them better – appreciating that they are just thoughts, not truths.

- Your mind becomes more attentive to the present moment, which helps you to focus better and become a better decision maker. It calms the thoughts in your head that preclude you from fully absorbing what is happening, be it a workplace presentation or a junior school play.

- Mindfulness helps you to understand and calm your emotions. Often, our emotions become so strong that they 'take over' and we lose the ability to think clearly or to respond in the best way to something. Mindfulness will help to reduce and eliminate these possibilities. It will help you to manage your feelings.

- Mindfulness meditation helps you to see things in a better perspective.

- Mindfulness helps you to learn to be at peace with yourself.

How does mindfulness work?

Mindfulness helps you to become calmly aware by helping you to pay attention to the present moment in a thoughtful and non-judgemental way. It achieves this by teaching you to practise a variety of meditation and breathing techniques that you will need to use on a daily basis in order to train your body and your mind to become accustomed to this new, stress-free, present state of being.

Remember this

There are a variety of books on mindfulness that you could chose to read and then follow the meditations described, or there are audio recordings to listen to in which a mindfulness teacher advises you on how best to meditate and follows the meditation through with you. But my recommendation would be to take a course. They are delightful experiences in themselves and you can share your experiences with others in a safe and peaceful environment.

The courses that are available are similar in style and content. They follow a set format and last eight weeks, with two hours of tutored experiential work a week followed by approximately one hour's practice a day at home, and one full day towards the end of the course to practise for a longer period the various new ways of being that you have learned. Wherever you live, it is likely that you will be able to find a course in basic MBSR or MBCBT within striking distance.

However, if you wish to try mindfulness at home, a few short and simple meditations are described below. They are daily practices that you could try as 'tasters'.

Remember this

Remember, the experience is simply whatever it is for you from moment to moment. You are not striving to achieve anything, to reach a goal. Just be still, with things as they are, in the present moment.

Try it now

This short Mindful Breathing meditation will take about ten minutes. First, make sure that you have the time to give to it and that you will not be interrupted.

Find somewhere comfortable to sit or lie down. You can sit in a chair or cross-legged on the floor, whichever you feel will help you to focus best. If you lie down, lie flat on your back with your legs straight. Try to keep your spine straight. If you are sitting, imagine that there is a string coming out of the top of your head that someone is gently pulling upwards. Or to put it another way, don't slouch!

Now begin to focus on your breathing and any sensations this creates. Be aware of the bodily movements involved in breathing – how your nostrils flare slightly, how your stomach rises and falls, how your breath moves round your body. Try to keep your focus of attention on your breathing. Notice any parts of your body where sensation arises, however slight. This will also help to keep you focused.

You will almost certainly find that your mind begins to wander after a while. You may not notice it at first but at some point you will have an awareness of your wandering thoughts. This in itself is a new experience: discovering the ability to (eventually) notice thoughts moving away from your focus and then to bring them back to your breathing meditation. Don't worry about this at all – it happens often and to everybody and is part of the meditation process. Gradually you will 'wander off' mentally for shorter periods before you become aware of what is happening and guide your thoughts back to your breathing.

Continue this breathing meditation for ten minutes (or thereabouts – you can use a timer or an alarm if you would like to be exact) and then gently open your eyes.

As it's a starter meditation, you may be curious about how you are 'supposed' to feel at the end of it: what are you 'supposed' to get out of it? The answer is simply that you get from it what you do. You have made a start at learning to *be* rather than to *do*, so well done. Be willing to accept whatever arises, good or bad, and keep practising. My hope for you, though, is that you will have felt peaceful and calm at the end of your meditation.

Remember this

If you find meditation boring, you can stop at any time. Use shorter time periods until you find a period that is right for you. Then extend it on occasions as you become more comfortable with it as a process. Or remind yourself that boredom is simply part of life; continue your meditation and notice whether the boredom passes once you have accepted it.

Try it now

Here are some suggestions for being mindful in a simple way in your everyday life. If you do nothing more than this, you will still be helping yourself to become calmer and more at peace.

✻ From the moment you wake up, and throughout the day, take the time to pay attention to your breathing for a short while. Focus fully on your breathing for a few moments and then return to what you were doing. Notice, as well, any bodily sensations and take a moment to examine them.

✻ Start eating and drinking mindfully. Take time over your food. Chew it well; savour and enjoy it; focus on it (don't read a book at the same time, for example). Do the same with any drink you are given or make for yourself. Be present with your food and drink, and focus on the pleasure it gives you.

✻ When you are walking anywhere, be aware of your posture, how your body feels, what muscles you are using and stretching. Focus on this rather than the thoughts buzzing round in your head.

✻ Ensure that any journeys you make by car or other transport are 'mindfully' taken. Give yourself a target, such as five things that you will notice on your journey that bring a smile to your face: children playing; a squirrel in a tree; someone proudly driving a new car. Be aware of your journey. As with the breathing meditation, if you find your thoughts wandering, bring them back to the moment and renew your awareness of the here and now.

✻ When you find yourself feeling impatient or frustrated, just return your mind to your breathing. Attempt to let go of any judgements you are making. Simply be aware of what is happening in an impartial way.

✻ Be as kind as you can, both to yourself and to others. Mindfulness generates warmth and compassion. It is a better way to be, and as you practise you will find it easier. Learn to forgive yourself for being a fallible human being and accept yourself as you are.

✻ Finally, as you settle into bed at night, once again focus on your breathing for a few minutes. Be aware of how your breathing slows when you focus on your abdomen rising and falling and when you are present in the moment rather than wandering off into the hinterlands of stressful thinking.

Focus points

* You will now be more familiar with the concept of mindfulness and how it may offer positive effectiveness in your life.

* You now understand it well enough to consider taking it further, either through more reading (the best books on mindfulness are by Dr Jon Kabat-Zinn), listening to audio recordings (Dr Kabat-Zinn has recorded an excellent CD set on mindfulness for beginners) or perhaps attending a course. There are recommendations at the end of the book of where you might find these.

* You have perhaps tried a brief mindfulness meditation for yourself. At the start, these can be confusing as there is a sense of 'I should be getting something specific from this' in most people's minds. It is hard to accept that you may find it difficult to identify this 'something' at the outset. Inner peace takes time and practice.

* Begin to incorporate mindful ways into your everyday life. As mindfulness becomes a habit it becomes easier and the release of stress eventually becomes visible.

Rate your effort (1–10) for the exercises you have tried in this chapter ......

Next step

As we near the end of this book, it would be remiss of me not to give some attention to the two most common mood disorders: depression and anxiety. Even if we are not sufferers ourselves, most of us will know someone who is. Many of these people have struggled for years and it is only in more recent times that help has become more widely available. CBT has proved an excellent treatment for these two disabling problems and its results in lifting mood and reducing anxiety are excellent.

If you have read this book out of general interest, rather than because you suffer at all from anxiety or depression, you may feel that you don't need to read these chapters. I leave this to you.

In Chapter 13, we look at depression.

Overcoming depression with CBT

Whether depression is a problem for you or you would just like to learn more about its treatment, by the end of this chapter you should:

▶ *have a greater understanding of the causes and maintenance of depressive symptoms*

▶ *have a greater understanding of the skills and techniques that will overcome depression.*

If you do not suffer from depression (your score above will give you an indication), this chapter is not essential reading. The skills used to defeat depression are a combination of many of the techniques you have learned earlier in this book, so you are not missing anything by leaving out this chapter.

How CBT can help with depression

It is possible that the reason you are reading this book is to discover how CBT can help you if you are suffering from depression or anxiety (covered in Chapters 14 and 15).

If this is the case and you would like to resolve issues that are troubling you, then – if you have worked through this book this far – you will now have all the skills that you need to recover from depression. However, learning more about depression specifically – what causes it, what maintains it and how to overcome it – will enhance your efforts.

First, I would like to help to normalize your problems. The more you know and understand about your difficulties, the less they will disturb you. Depression is simply a mood disorder – and you have now learned a lot about moods and what triggers them and changes them. You may be able to point to events in your life that are negative and distressing, believing that these events are the cause of your depression. But this is not the case; depression is actually caused by the way you view these events and how this makes you feel – by your thoughts and perceptions about specific events, about yourself, about life in general and about the future.

This chapter will offer you thoughts and ideas to develop your thinking about negative areas of your life and to encourage you to see your difficulties as challenges that you can overcome with effort and perseverance. If you do suffer from depression, you are not alone. Dr Paul Gilbert, in his book *Overcoming Depression*, suggests that there may be over 300 million people in the world today who suffer from it.

Depression is occasionally described as the 'common cold' of psychological disorders, and GPs say that approximately one in three of the patients they see will have some sort of depressive symptoms.

Key idea

Depression is a very distressing illness, and the feelings of bleakness and hopelessness it gives rise to need not be supported – there is a better way to live.

Am I depressed?

Many people live for years with the symptoms of depression without being aware of them. Where depression is chronic (i.e. it has lasted a very long time), individuals lose track of what balanced thinking is and their pessimistic outlook seems a correct assessment of life to them.

For others, depression is a sudden onslaught of negativity that hits like a blunt instrument and there can be no doubt that things have gone badly wrong emotionally. Understandably, this can be frightening.

There are recognized signs of depression and the chapter self-assessment questions highlighted some of these and enabled you to get some idea of your mood levels. If this initial assessment does suggest that you may be a sufferer, look at the list below of the indicators of depression that are common in most cases. Use the rating of 1–3 you used in the self-assessment test to measure the extent to which any of the symptoms might apply to you. Also, if you recognize symptoms, ask yourself how long you have felt this way. Everyone has low periods but these are only classed as depression when they fail to disappear over a reasonable period of time; then it is time either to seek help or to help yourself.

1 Feelings of guilt, worthlessness or hopelessness.

2 Difficulty in sleeping and waking up early.

3 Finding that the start of the day is the worst, and feeling somewhat better in the evening.

4 Extreme tiredness, with no energy and possibly little appetite.

5 Weight loss.

6 Headaches, abdominal pains and palpitations.

7 Anxiety, panic attacks, overwhelming sadness, bouts of crying.

8 Inability to make decisions, feeling inadequate and unable to cope.

9 Feelings of isolation and insecurity.

10 Feeling guilty that you cannot cope, that you are not meeting expectations, both your own and those of others.

Count up your rating. A score of 20–30 indicates depression; a score of 10–20 would be more accurately described as 'low mood'.

These scores are a rough guide, of course, as there are variations in levels of depression over time. For example, many people find that they feel their worst in the morning, when any measurement would be very high, but that they feel much better in the evening, when their rating would be much lower.

If your combined scores for the self-assessment test and the assessment above are very high, i.e. a combined total of 40–45, I do suggest that you consider seeking professional help from your GP, who will be able to arrange both depression-reducing medication and psychological therapy to help you. However, if your combined score is lower than this, you should be able to tackle this yourself using CBT skills and techniques.

What causes depression?

I am asked this frequently by my clients and they are understandably disappointed to hear me say that there is no one specific cause that we can pinpoint. There are various elements that may trigger depression on their own or come together to do so. These elements can include nature/nurture – from a genetic disposition to a difficult upbringing – or they might include events in adult life that lead to specific or on-going trauma. In the fast-paced world of the 21st century, stress also plays a great part in triggering depression.

Sometimes, a specific event or series of events – perhaps the loss of a loved one followed by a house move or job loss, for example – can trigger depression and we call this *event-specific*, as it is usually easy to identify the trigger and to work with how to come to terms with it and move forward from it, after which the depression normally recedes.

However, it can sometimes be hard to find a specific cause for feeling so wretched and this makes things even worse – to be living a life that seems to have little in it that is negative and yet to feel so terrible is the hardest thing.

A further type of depression is chronic depression, when the sufferer can scarcely recall a time when everything felt less than flat and hopeless.

All of these types of depression respond well to CBT, so I want to reassure you that you are not 'different' from anyone else and you will have as much success in defeating depression if you work at it as anyone else.

THE ROLE OF THOUGHTS AND BELIEFS

Think back to what you learned at the start of the book about the elements that come together to give us information about what is causing or maintaining our problems. You will recall that these can be:

► cognitive

► emotional

► physical

► behavioural.

What we referred to above as event-specific depression is most likely to be caused by negative automatic thoughts (NATs) – seeing the event(s) in a negative, pessimistic way. Non-specific or chronic depression is more likely to be maintained by core beliefs that the individual has held for a long time – perhaps always. Such faulty beliefs, as you now know, drive assumptions, rules for living and behaviours. This in turn means that the thinking style of sufferers, while seeming rather gloomy to others, makes complete sense to them and is quite rational.

So now you will appreciate how we need a variety of skills and techniques at different levels of thinking in order to encourage our brains towards a more balanced view.

WILL I ALWAYS HAVE DEPRESSION?

No. Depression can be cured with psychological help, and sometimes medicinal help as well. Even when people make no effort at all to get over depression, after a period of time it will disappear of its own accord. However, this period of time can be shortened by actively engaging in working to get rid of it.

Overcoming depression

You already have all the tools you need in your 'toolbox' and in this section we will bring out the right ones to help you.

CONCEPTUALIZING DEPRESSION

Your best way forward is to draw up a simple conceptualization of what is going on. Remember your mantra: 'What you think decides how you feel.' So your first step is to look at your thinking. You will immediately see that not only does what you think decide how you feel, but in depression how you feel decides what you think. What you think and feel then usually controls your behavioural decisions. If you feel tired and flat, you are unlikely to do very much.

Try it now

Return to Chapter 3, when we first drew up a conceptualization, or 'map', of what's going on. Now draw this out for yourself and place within it what you were thinking and feeling, how you felt physically and what you did behaviourally. Look at the two-way arrows. Can you see how your thoughts tend to drive the other parts of the conceptualization? Can you then see how the other elements feed back into your thoughts so that they become even more negative?

BREAKING OUT OF THE DEPRESSION SPIRAL

Your low mood and negative thinking affect your physiology, so that you feel tired and lethargic. This in turn affects your behaviour, which will probably also become negative as you do less and less. As you study the spiral, think about how it might apply to you, and to how you deal with your own problems. Does it seem familiar in any way? Tackling it from either a cognitive or behavioural starting point will help you begin to lift your mood.

You understand enough now about thought-challenging to know that first you need to start by working on seeing things in a more balanced way. Start with your thoughts. Eventually you may see a pattern to your thinking that will throw up a few negative beliefs that you had been unaware of, and then you can begin to work with them. But for the moment, focus on your thinking.

Try it now

Your best way to challenge and change these thoughts, as you already know, is by using a Thought Record. Since you are familiar with the process, you can use a full, seven-column Thought Record. Look not only at biased thinking but also at patterns of thinking that may throw up unhelpful beliefs.

Fill in your Thought Record on a regular basis, starting immediately and providing at least two or three investigations on a daily basis. As always, write everything down. Review your Thought Record after week one. Can you see any positive changes appearing? These changes may be as simple as 'I don't find it so hard to look for evidence now' or 'I am beginning to believe my alternative thoughts just a little more often'. You don't need to see ground-breaking changes; even the smallest ones will be extremely productive at the moment.

Remember this

Because negative thoughts are particularly severe in depression, you will need to use your 'where's the evidence?' question extremely strongly and make sure that you always write something in your evidence columns rather than feeling that there is nothing to put down. Your depression will fight you, so persevere. Beat it

▶ Interpreting your Thought Record

You have worked with Thought Records a lot now so you should be able to glean a great deal of information from the one you have just created for yourself. Look out for the following.

▶ Can you find any evidence of faulty thinking styles? Refer back to Chapter 5 to remind yourself of these. It will help you to realize the distorted thinking bias you are using without having to search too hard on your own. Then you can revisit the thought and redevelop it in a more balanced way.

▶ Can you find any patterns of thinking that might help you identify any negative beliefs that are operating?

For example, if you find yourself having thoughts with a pattern such as 'I've got things wrong again' or 'Everything I try ends up badly', you could be activating an 'I'm worthless' belief. Once you identify a negative belief, you can work on replacing it with one that is more helpful.

▶ Both thoughts and beliefs are important

Depression is often activated by long-held beliefs, so digging these out and working with them is very important. (Refer back to Chapter 9 if you need to jog your memory about how to achieve this.) If you work only with negative thoughts and challenging these, you will find yourself stuck when your more optimistic view flies in the face of the negative beliefs that you hold. You will never be able to adjust your thinking if you haven't already adjusted your belief(s).

For example, if your negative thought, after someone ignores you at a party is 'They obviously didn't like me', a balanced alternative might be 'I doubt it was personal, they seemed in a hurry'. This may work well as long as it is not trying to override an 'I'm completely worthless' belief, which it never will. When you believe something strongly, any alternative thoughts will carry no weight. So first you need to make some sort of belief shift – perhaps, in this case, to something like 'I have less worth than many but more than some'. To reiterate, do notice how the alternative response is *close* to the original negative belief. It is not so far away as to be unbelievable. This is a 'chipping away' process so that you are always able to feel that there is an element of possible validity in the new belief you are creating. As you search for evidence to support this new belief, you may be able to move your belief even further. Take it one step at a time and you will gradually consolidate a much more helpful way of evaluating situations.

Overcoming the physical effects

Depression is exhausting. It saps your energy completely and leaves you feeling lethargic and tired even from the moment you wake up. Feeling tired is likely to keep your mood low and discourages you from being active. Motivation to do anything disappears. It is replaced by flatness and lack of interest in anything much. All this in turn feeds the depression. So what can you do when you feel exhausted but know that this isn't helping things at all?

Although the most attractive option is often to stay home, which feels much easier and safer, this is going to maintain your depression. The less you do, the less you want to do. So getting active, even when it is the last thing in the world that you feel like, is a vital component of recovery.

I do understand how immensely difficult this can be. But I also know that depression is so debilitating, so life-reducing, that stretching yourself to attempt things that seem difficult is a *far* better option than living with this disabling disorder.

RECORDING ACTIVITIES

A basic CBT tool in dealing with inactivity in depression and its negative repercussions is an Activity Schedule. Activity Schedules serve two clear purposes.

1 As with a Thought Record, once you start to record what you are doing as well as what you are thinking, you tend to find the motivation to build a little more activity into your day.

2 It helps you to identify when you feel at your worst, at your best and just OK. This can give you valuable information about your patterns of depression and what might trigger an especially low mood, giving you the power to make changes.

Key idea

The drawback of Activity Schedules is that they can seem a bothersome bore, especially when even the most interesting activities fail to arouse your interest. Using your thought-challenging skills can help you. For example:

Event: Filling in an Activity Schedule

NAT: This is extremely boring and dull. I just can't be bothered.

Alternative: The reason everything seems boring just now is due to my depression. There is a point to activity scheduling. I can give this a chance for just a few days and see if it is helpful in fighting my low mood.

Try it now

Take a sheet of paper and rule eight lines down the page. The first column needs to contain the time of day, marked off in hourly divisions – 9 a.m., 10 a.m., and so on, for the whole day. The other seven columns are the days of the week. Write into your schedule immediately any activities that you already have scheduled. If your Activity Schedule looks rather blank, ask yourself what else you might do to fill it up. Make a real effort here.

It should look something like the example below. Admittedly, rather dull but also very important. Put a cross against the times and situations when you feel at your lowest. Put a tick against the times you feel at your best.

Time	Monday	Tuesday	Wednesday	Thursday	Friday	Saturday	Sunday
7 a.m. Rate mood	Get up, wash and dress	Get up, wash and dress	Get up, wash and dress	Get up, wash and dress	Get up, wash and dress	Lie in	Lie in
8 a.m. Rate mood	Take children to school	Take children to school	Take children to school	Take children to school	Take children to school	Get up	Get up
9 a.m. Rate mood	Go to work	Go to work	Day off – go to shopping centre and see friend for lunch	Go to work	Wait in for repair man	Take children to swimming class	Walk dog, then take children to grandparents

Activity Schedule

Try it now

Do you begin to see patterns in when you feel good and when you feel low? What do you make of this? What information do these patterns give you? Write down your discoveries.

Now think about what you might do with what you have discovered.

Remember this

Don't let yourself fall for the old 'When I feel more up to it I'll do this' error. You need to do the opposite. Doing something when you don't feel up to it will gradually help you to feel up to it.

USING EXERCISE TO IMPROVE YOUR MOOD

In Chapter 10, we extolled the benefits of physical exercise as a mood enhancer. Now here it is again. Your Activity Schedule can include anything and everything, from a trip round the shops to a visit to the dentist. However, physical activity of the type that requires you to put on a pair of trainers is also essential. I advise some of my clients to 'do the freebies first', i.e. start exercising and improve your diet. These things cost nothing, so don't embark on expensive help before you have tried out what might help you at no cost.

You may have heard of the brain chemical serotonin, which is regarded as one of our mood regulators; the more serotonin we have, the better we feel. Regular exercise will provide your brain with a natural boost of serotonin. Think of distance runners coming up to the winning post. As they cross it they should collapse with exhaustion. Instead, they are skipping and jumping, full of energy and happiness. This is due to the serotonin their exercise has manufactured. It gives them a natural 'high'.

Key idea

Physical exercise is one of the best mood lifters available.

Adjusting your behaviours

Many of my clients are nervous of behavioural change. For this reason, it is usually last on the list of things to work on to alleviate depression. Working on cognitions seems a less nerve-racking first option. However, at some point behavioural change is an essential component of overcoming depression. Some of these behavioural changes will be obvious, such as getting out more, socializing, working, gardening – whatever increases your activity and energy levels. Other changes may require you to face up to difficult situations that you had perhaps been avoiding, and these are much harder to do. A helpful tool is to test things out.

Instead of feeling that you are making a major commitment to long-term changes that you may or may not like, regard changes as short-term experiments. Try something different and see what happens. These behavioural experiments can be difficult to begin with, as they require courage from you to test a hypothesis that you won't believe in. You will initially be expecting a negative result, not a positive one.

However, you can set yourself up to succeed by taking manageable steps. Look back at the sections on goal-setting in Chapter 2 and behavioural experiments in Chapter 8. As you saw there, the most encouraging way forward is to take small steps that will give you a sense of achievement, rather than giant steps that are more likely to meet with failure.

For example, to test a belief that you are dull and uninteresting, you may need to try starting up conversations with people to see if you are right. You can start in a small way. Perhaps just making a one-sentence comment to the assistant behind the shop counter such as 'That's a nice display of fruit you have', or 'Isn't it hot for October?'. Note how people respond to your efforts. Decide what you make of this and how it fits with your beliefs about yourself. Be curious and interested. Use the SMART model to set your goals and you will gradually gain more and more confidence, which in turn will encourage a positive mood change.

Research in different continents, among different nationalities and over long periods of time has shown that the greatest mood lifter around is the least used. What is it? Altruism. Test it out. Try doing something kind for someone less fortunate than you and see how you feel afterwards.

Focus points

* You will now appreciate that depression is a mood disorder and one that many people suffer from. It is a problem that can be cured using CBT skills and techniques, which become skills for life.
* If you feel that depression or low mood may be a problem for you, have confidence that you now have the skills for a programme of recovery.
* Ensure that your efforts are organized and plan well. Start out by looking at your thinking and beliefs and don't start changing

behaviours until you feel more comfortable with the idea that it is worthwhile.

✽ Don't get discouraged too quickly. As with many things, the groundwork takes time and the results may be slow to come at first. But gradually you will become more familiar with the strategies you are using and the positive results will start. So please don't give up.

✽ For most people, small, consistent steps forward will be more beneficial than occasional larger ones punctured by periods of withdrawal and inactivity.

If depression is something you suffer from and you have worked on the exercises in this chapter, rate your effort (1–10) for the exercises you have tried ......

Next step

Anxiety has recently been described as 'the new depression'. There is much truth in this. As life becomes faster paced and more stressful, the number of people who cope with a variety of different levels and types of stress and anxiety has increased greatly. This may be due in part to the fact that people are willing to talk more openly about their difficulties now than in past years, when it was less acceptable.

Anxiety is a large umbrella that covers a wide variety of disorders, from generalized anxiety to obsessive compulsive disorder (OCD), with panic, phobia, social anxiety, health anxiety and a myriad other difficulties in between.

If you are suffering in any way from stress or worry, Chapters 14 and 15 can offer considerable help.

Defeating anxiety

If anxiety is a problem for you, by the end of this chapter you should understand:

▶ *what maintains and increases anxiety*

▶ *what the simple errors are that people make in trying to reduce anxiety*

▶ *several techniques for overcoming anxiety.*

In recent times anxiety has been called 'the new depression'. With fast-paced, stressful lives, anxiety about 'What if' scenarios is never far away and very many people suffer from it. Anxiety is especially distressing because of the physical impact it has on the sufferer: stomach churning, heart pounding, giddiness, sweating – a wide variety of symptoms that are not only frighteningly unpleasant in themselves but which can lead many anxiety sufferers to think that they are extremely ill. Indeed, it is the physical symptoms of anxiety that cause people the most worry and raise their anxiety levels even further. An assumption is made that to feel so bad must be a sign that something is seriously wrong.

Remember this

Meta anxiety is what we call 'feeling anxious about feeling anxious', and it drives our panicky feelings up even further. It means that instead of an event or perceptions of an event making us anxious, the mere thought of being anxious makes us even more anxious! This is an important (rather than simply an amusing) point, so do bear it in mind as you learn more about overcoming this problem.

What causes anxiety?

Think about the last few times you were highly anxious about something. What went through your mind?

The chances are that you thought in terms of:

- possible catastrophe
- the catastrophe being unbearable for you
- a complete inability on your part to cope with this catastrophe
- lack of help from others, perhaps leading to embarrassment on top of everything else.

When we are in an anxious frame of mind, not only do we expect a 'worst-case scenario', but we may also conclude that it would be quite unbearable . We then convince ourselves that we would be completely unable to cope if this dreaded event came about, and we believe it more likely that people would stand by and watch, rather than help, if our feared worry happened in front of others. This is another example of a phrase you are now familiar with: 'faulty thinking'.

Along with faulty thinking, we experience physical sensations so strong and so hard to tolerate that 'in the moment' the negative prediction seems very real and likely, rather than exaggerated and unlikely.

Of course, anxiety isn't always a bad thing. Anxiety is what prevents us from walking in front of buses, or driving over cliff edges. It keeps us safe. So we are not trying to get rid of anxiety, as that would be dangerous. What we need to be able to do is recognize *appropriate* and *inappropriate* anxiety and how to tell the difference between the two.

For example, if you were travelling on a train and it came to a shuddering halt for no apparent reason, then becoming slightly nervous about what this meant – perhaps wondering if the train had broken down and what this would mean for your plans – would be appropriate to the situation. However, if your reaction to the train stopping is that it was about to be boarded by terrorists who would kill you all, then your anxiety would rise to an inappropriately high level and you might even have a panic attack. In the second instance, your 'catastrophizing' faulty thinking kicks in, releasing hard-to-tolerate physical symptoms that in turn increase your anxiety levels.

Don't worry about appropriate anxiety. It is giving you important information that you may need to act on (such as, in the example above, ringing a friend to tell them you will be late). Only when anxiety is clearly inappropriate to situations (even to you, in calmer moments) and is spoiling your life, do you need to do something about it.

If we are depressed we usually trawl back through the past in a negative way or see the present moment as without hope or meaning. Anxiety, on the other hand, causes us to ruminate about events that have not *actually* happened and that may not happen.

ANXIETY'S ATTEMPTS TO HELP

As mentioned earlier, our first response to the physical sensations of anxiety, especially as they get worse the more worried we become, is often that we will pass out, be physically sick or possibly even have a heart attack and die. It seems obvious to us that our body is harming us. Yet the contrary is true – it is actually trying to helping us!

To understand how and why, you need to think back to the time of the caveman. Fighting off wild animals while gathering enough food to feed the family meant life was very dangerous. So the body developed the 'fight or flight' mechanism, so that in the face of danger an urgent message is sent from the brain to the body, and the body responds appropriately. When danger threatens, messages pass from the brain to different parts of the body telling it to speed up and be prepared for extra activity. Extra adrenaline is pumped round it, more blood sent to the muscles, and the heart rate speeded up – everything that you may experience when you get anxious. This actually had a purpose at that time, making the caveman strong enough to either fight or run (his choice). For example, if you sometimes feel a little dizzy or light-headed when you get anxious, this is because your body is taking blood from your head (where it considers you don't need it in a dangerous situation) and passing it to your leg and arm muscles (which it considers need the extra blood supply in these circumstances). This bodily reaction is called 'autonomic arousal'. It is simply the normal bodily response to danger or threat in the world about us.

In the present day there are still frightening situations and threats but they rarely require you to engage in physical force. The things that disturb us now are more likely to worry us psychologically than physically. Yet our body still responds to danger messages from the brain in the same way it has always done. In a sense, it is many thousands of years out of date!

How do you feel when you become anxious? What sensations do you notice?

Perhaps some of the following may be familiar.

▶ **Poor concentration and memory.** When you are under stress, thoughts may become fuzzy and hard to organize. You can become easily distracted or can't take in or remember information as effectively as normal.

▶ **Sleep disturbance.** Worry can make it particularly difficult to 'switch off' and sleep is often affected. This has a build-up effect that gets worse over an extended period of time.

▶ **Short temper, irritability.** If you are experiencing excessive worry and tiredness, you may find you become more easily frustrated and have little energy for problems outside your most immediate concerns. This can make you snappy and short-tempered.

▶ **Tiredness and lethargy.** Worry and tension use up a lot of energy so that it feels difficult to make the effort to cope.

▶ **Depression.** The feeling that worries are taking over your life or disrupting normal activities can lead to feelings of depression and despair. This, in turn, often makes it difficult to believe that change is possible or that life can be better. Your motivation goes and you no longer feel like doing the things you once enjoyed.

Remember this

Although these may seem to be worrying symptoms, they are simply alerting you to the fact that your thinking has become conditioned to look at things in an anxious way. The symptoms are not harmful in themselves, nor are they indications of any serious physical or emotional problems.

THE ANXIETY SPIRAL

We have already touched on the way that anxiety spirals out of control. Worrying thoughts lead to physical sensations that worry us even more and encourage us to see the situation as even worse than we previously thought it was. This then causes an even higher level of anxiety. This spiral can continue for some people until they have a full-blown panic attack.

Key idea

Do keep in mind the idea of a 'spiral'. This is important as it enables you to understand why your anxiety can get worse. It isn't (necessarily) that the situation has got worse but simply that your thoughts and sensations are bouncing back and forth between each other, driving the anxiety upwards.

Maintaining behaviours

We always try to act in our own best interests, and it seems sensible and natural when we feel highly anxious to do whatever seems likely to us to get rid of the anxiety. For example, someone who fears having a panic attack on a train never travels on one. Someone who fears that they blush when spoken to avoids contact with others as much as possible. If you think you will do very badly in a competition, best not to even enter. These seem like obvious, natural solutions to our fears and worries, and what is more, they seem to work so we continue doing them. As you know, we call these 'safety behaviours' as we believe that they are actions that keep us safe.

But the downside to adopting safety behaviours is that we never discover that our worries might have been without foundation. So we maintain our faulty belief that something terrible will happen and we won't be able to cope. We never discover that, in all probability, the 'something terrible' won't actually happen, or that if it did we would deal with it. When I ask a client, 'What is the worst thing that could happen?', they often answer 'I don't know. I never get that far with my thinking. As soon as I feel anxious I use a safety behaviour.'

Unless you are prepared to consider the worst-case scenario, you cannot develop a plan for dealing with it. So the 'I won't be able to cope' faulty thinking is maintained.

Remember this

'One ought never to turn one's back on a threatened danger and try to run away from it. If you do that, you will double the danger. But if you meet it promptly and without flinching, you will reduce the danger by half. Never run away from anything. Never!

Sir Winston Churchill, British prime minister 1940–5 and 1951–5

AVOIDANCE

The most common safety behaviour is avoidance, and I've described some situations above where avoidance seems to make sense. 'Oh, but I don't avoid situations. I always face up to them, yet nothing changes' is a common response. However, when we examine what is going on, 'facing up to' a social function, for example, can still trigger safety behaviours, such as not staying for long or sitting quietly in the hope that no one will talk to you.

Your avoidance behaviour may be more subtle than you realize. Are you really facing your fears fully, or only partially?

ESCAPE

As with avoidance, escape involves giving something your best shot, but the moment that you feel even a smidgeon of anxiety rising within you, it's time to go. Feeling panicky in the cinema? Look for the emergency exit, get into the street and gulp down some fresh air. Thank goodness for that!

Sometimes, escapees will plan ahead for their escape. They will ensure that they have the aisle seat in the school play or sit by the emergency exit in the concert hall. This helps them feel more relaxed, but again, the thinking is maintaining the problem not solving it. Rather than adopting an anxiety-reducing approach ('Even *if* I get anxious, I am sure I will be all right'), they are maintaining the problem by expecting to be anxious ('*When* I get anxious, I can leave easily before it escalates')

What is the difference between being inside the room and outside in the street? Why do you feel panicky in one place and relaxed in the other? Is it the air? Is it the temperature? Become curious about what the difference actually is. In one place you feel you are about to have a major anxiety attack and a few yards away you are completely relaxed. And there is the key, of course. The word 'relaxed'. You cannot be both anxious and relaxed at the same time. The moment you no longer fear disaster, all is well.

LOOKING TOO CLOSELY

If you think you felt your heart wobble strangely or that you heard a funny noise in the dark outside, what do you do? You focus. You turn all your attention towards whatever it is that seems unnerving and concentrate on it. Up to a point, this is a good thing. But what happens when you have been reassured – the doctor says your heart is fine, or your partner goes out with a torch and reports a flower pot falling off a ledge? You still cannot relax. Your faulty thinking tells you that the fact you are still anxious means that the danger is still there. So you sit and listen to your heartbeat constantly. You go on the internet and look up heart-related sensations. Your view becomes that you need to be hyper-vigilant to ensure that you stay safe. But this hyper-vigilance is itself exhausting and keeps your anxiety level high.

The essence of overcoming anxiety

The strategies needed to eliminate inappropriate anxiety have already been set out in this book and now you need to pick those that offer the most appropriate approach to deal with this particular problem. These are summarized below, but first please ensure that the following two paragraphs are engraved on your heart before you start work.

▶ The biggest mistake that most people make when trying to rid themselves of worry and anxiety is to feel that reducing the physical symptoms is the goal. But this will achieve nothing as you already have lots of ways of reducing your anxiety (all those safety behaviours!) and none of them work.

▶ The key to overcoming anxiety is to focus on reducing the strength of the erroneous belief that keeps the anxiety so high.

When you reduce your fear of what might happen by cognitive and behavioural testing, your anxiety will go away of its own accord. You need do nothing to bring it down; it will bring itself down. So make your focus in this chapter and Chapter 15 to work on testing your beliefs and reducing their strength. Think of the analogy of Darth Vader, in his huge black cloak being faced down by tiny Luke Skywalker. When Luke stood up to Vader, he reduced him to a pile of ashes. Think of your anxiety in this way. It seems like a huge and terrifying thing but really it is just a pile of ashes.

CHALLENGING ANXIOUS THINKING

With anxiety, the most common thinking error is to see things as more dangerous than they are. So your more balanced thinking needs to focus on looking for a less threatening alternative explanation for your worries. For example, if you are extremely anxious about the fact that your boss has asked to see you, you might counter your negative predictions about the reasons for this by reminding yourself that you have been commended for your work on several occasions recently. Or you could say to yourself, 'Well, if he is going to give me the sack, so be it. I am very employable and will quickly find a job I like better'. You will notice that the first thought suggestion offers an alternative to your negative anxiety (the over-estimation of catastrophe) while the second suggestion helps you to see that even if the worst came to the worst, you would cope (under-estimating your coping skills).

BEHAVIOURAL TESTING

Work first with cognitions to begin to give yourself confidence and to loosen the strength of some of your fears. Once you have achieved this you need to be brave enough to test out the validity of your anxious thoughts, and to do this you need to make a plan.

As ever, the Thought Record is a key aid in assisting you with this. With anxiety, you are dealing with your predictions about the likelihood of future events, rather than trying to evaluate the past or present. So look at your Behavioural Experiment Thought Record, as this is the format to use to test an anxious prediction. With your Behavioural Experiment Thought Record in front of you, write in:

1 **What I am going to do**

   This means making a decision to test a negative assumption. Suppose you fear that if you go in a lift you will have a panic attack. Then you will need to make a step-by-step plan to test this out. You will recall 'graded exposure', discussed in Chapter 8; perhaps Step 1 might be simply to wait by the entrance to the lift in the shopping mall.

2 **What do I predict is the worst thing that could happen?**

   Here you are going to write down your worst-case scenario. It might be: 'Even standing near a lift will make me feel nervous and shaky. I could see myself passing out.'

3 **What actually happened?**

   Well? What happened?! Here is a guesstimate for the example I have used. 'I did feel nervous but the longer I stood there, the more relaxed I got. I managed to stand by the lift for 10 minutes and then it simply seemed rather boring.'

4 What have I learned from this?

Here, an answer might be: 'I was quite nervous, but it wasn't nearly as bad as I thought it would be and I found that the longer I stayed the more my anxiety levels dropped.'

5 How can I build on this?

This is where you plan your 'next step'. You might decide, in view of your initial anxiety, to do this exercise once or twice more before moving on, or you might be keen to take a further step: perhaps entering the lift while it is stationary, or even travelling up just one floor. You will make your decisions here based on your increasing confidence.

Try it now

Create your own Behavioural Experiment Thought Record. Write it up as far as you can and now have a 'trial run'. Pick something simple that doesn't cause you too much anxiety and behaviourally test it out. See what happens and record your findings on your Thought Record. What have you learned from this?

ANOTHER SKILL: THEORY A AND THEORY B

This theory invites the anxious person to consider two alternative propositions.

▶ the first (Theory A) is that his or her fears are correct and that the problem is therefore one of catastrophe. For example, 'If I drive on a motorway, I will have a panic attack that will cause me to have a stroke'.

▶ the second (Theory B) is that the problem is possibly not one of disaster, but one of *worry* about disaster. For example, 'I *worry* that I might panic, and that this might cause me to have a stroke'.

You can write both ideas up alongside each other which will give you greater clarity about the difference between them. Here is an example:

Theory A possibility	Theory B possibility
If I go to the cinema, once it goes dark and I am trapped inside, I will have a panic attack which will cause a major disturbance and possibly kill me.	If I go to the cinema, I worry that once it goes dark and I am trapped inside, I will have a panic attack which will cause a major disturbance and possibly kill me.
Evidence for this view: I have felt as though something terrible could happen when I have been to the cinema in the past.	*Evidence for this view:* My thoughts do make me extremely anxious, but nothing physically bad has ever happened, nor have I heard of this happening to anyone else.
What I need to do if this is true: Never again go to the cinema and warn all my friends of the possible consequences to them of going to the cinema.	*What I need to do if this is true:* Take steps to learn to reduce my anxiety and face my fears. I need to go to the cinema more often until I am comfortable.

Key idea

When I put the above proposition to my clients and ask them which theory they subscribe to, Theory A or Theory B, they generally say, 'Oh, Theory B, of course. I realize that it's just worry'. It is as though I have wasted their time asking too simple a question. They understand the point of Theory A/Theory B only when I then ask them: 'If you know that this is a problem of worry, why do you treat it as a problem of danger?'. We are then able to work together using the skills and techniques for resolving anxiety and they are happier to drop their safety behaviours – especially when I tell them that if they believe in Theory A, their homework will be to warn all their friends against going to the cinema, or whatever!

VISUALIZATION

Some people's anxiety is so bad with regard to a particular feared situation that the thought of beginning any form of behavioural testing is too much for them to contemplate. This is often the situation in the case of agoraphobia, where someone is too frightened to leave their house. In these circumstances they can use visualizing as a technique and start by simply imagining themselves opening the front door instead of actually doing it. As you might think, the technique involves sitting quietly and 'turning on a television' in your mind. You then picture yourself doing whatever it is that you are fearful of. Some of my clients find that even this brings on anxious feelings very quickly, so begin with small challenges and work towards the more difficult. As always, don't set yourself up to fail. Imagine easy things to start with, and don't move on until you can hold the image for some time and feel comfortable with it. Equally, if the image is stressful, step backwards metaphorically speaking and find something less anxiety-provoking to start with.

SYMPTOM RELIEF

Many CBT practitioners lean towards regarding relaxation and deep breathing (discussed in Chapter 11) as a further example of safety behaviours. Rightfully, they argue that the goal is not to learn how to relax more next time you feel a panic attack coming on but for you not to have any more panic attacks. There is a lot of merit in this argument. My own view, however, is that early in your quest to overcome anxiety you will find yourself in situations in which everything you have learned goes out of the window. Having symptom relief to use in these cases may be a saviour. Understand that these are only symptom relief, not problem solvers. But use them when you feel that you really need to – make an informed decision and you will be fine as long as you don't abandon the more important work of ensuring that your anxiety is eventually banished for good.

! Focus points

* We have looked at the causes of anxiety and what maintains it. You should now have a much better idea of the detrimental effects of safety behaviours, useful though they seem. Unless you drop them, they will simply reinforce your anxiety and you will not overcome it.

* When using a Thought Record to rethink your anxiety worries, consider always that you are looking for a less threatening explanation for your fears in order to help them subside.

* Have more confidence in your own coping skills. You can stand your ground and nothing bad will happen to you. Your anxiety will go away of its own accord.

* Devising behavioural experiments to test the validity of your worries will help you to overcome them. Don't set yourself up to fail; use graded exposure to take small steps that will give you confidence and keep you motivated.

If you suffer from anxiety and have done the exercises in this chapter, rate your effort (1–10) for the exercises you have tried ......

Next step

You will now have a much better idea of how anxiety arises generally and how we often erroneously maintain it – or make it worse – rather than reducing it. You may, however, find that you are only anxious in specific areas of your life. Perhaps you have phobic anxiety, such as fear of snakes or spiders or getting on a plane; or perhaps a fear of confined spaces, such as lifts or train compartments in which you may have a panic attack. Or possibly you have obsessive compulsive disorder (OCD), with thoughts that don't make sense to others and inspire actions such as relentless checking or handwashing that seem vital to you to prevent something bad happening. Chapter 15 deals with a variety of these specific anxiety disorders and explains how to eliminate them.

Dealing with anxiety disorders

Chapter 14 looked at anxiety as a general concept. This chapter considers anxiety that is specific to one area of someone's life. By the end of this chapter you should:

▶ *know more about specific types of anxiety*

▶ *understand what maintains the problems*

▶ *understand what skills and techniques can be used to overcome the problems.*

Even if you do not have a problem with any of these, a good understanding of them will make you far more empathetic to those who do. Most of these anxiety types are extremely common, but people shy away from owning up to them.

Self-assessment

1 Would you describe yourself as generally 'a worrier'?

2 If so, does this bother you, or do you feel that worrying helps as it keeps you on the alert for mishap and danger?

3 Do you have any irrational worries that don't seem to bother others; for example, a fear of heights, spiders, etc.

4 Have you ever had what felt like a panic attack? That is, anxiety that seemed to be getting completely out of control, leaving you frightened of the outcome.

5 Are you 'particular' about things, i.e. certain types of order are important to you, you like to check on things several times, scrupulous cleanliness is important to you? Does this behaviour bother you, but do you feel powerless to stop it?

If you have answered 'yes' to any of the above questions, you may be someone whose anxiety is very focused in a particular area. While many people tolerate their idiosyncratic worries, for other people these can be at best a nuisance and at worst something that plays havoc with their lives.

It is common for people to suffer from anxiety that is very specific to one area of their life. Examples might be health anxiety – where an individual is happy and relaxed in most situations but worries over every twitch and tingle and what it might mean – or social anxiety, where someone who is normally calm and intelligent and good at their job finds any type of social or interactive occasion a trauma.

If these problems seriously affect your life, it would be best for you to seek professional help. However, if the problems are mild, the skills and techniques in this chapter may be enough to deal with them successfully. As you can now apply the basic

CBT skills and techniques covered in this book, this chapter will not go over these but will add to this basic knowledge some more specific key facts and treatment possibilities.

Generalized anxiety disorder

Let's start with Generalized Anxiety Disorder (GAD). Many of us suffer from this, or if we don't ourselves, then we know someone who does, worrying all day long about anything and everything. Indeed, they don't seem to be happy if they are *not* worrying; antennae out all the time, metaphorically patrolling and on constant lookout, they feel that they need to do all this to prevent possible disaster.

Because GAD is a generalized anxiety, sufferers find that as one worry goes, another comes along to fill its place. It is not the events that are the problem, but the sufferer's consistent perception of such events as threats and problems.

Case study

Here's an example of how GAD can affect people.

Jenny was 52 and felt that she really ought to be very happy about her life. After marrying late, she and her husband James had produced two beautiful children through IVF. James had a good job as a partner in a law firm and they had a lovely home. Jenny was able to follow activities and pursuits that she enjoyed and she gained enormous pleasure from being a mum to her son and daughter.

Idyllic though this sounds, Jenny spent so much of her time worrying that she failed to enjoy any of it. Supposing James lost his job? Supposing the children didn't get into the schools they were hoping for? How would she cope when her parents died? Should she be spending more time cleaning the house and less time socializing? Should she be spending less time cleaning the house and more time helping her son and daughter with their homework?

Life seemed like one long battle to Jenny, and she could not remember a time when worry had not dominated it. Yet strangely, although all this worrying prevented Jenny from relaxing and enjoying life as it was, she saw it as helpful and necessary rather than something to be overcome. Jenny thought that the more she worried, the more likely it would be that a solution would pop up that would resolve everything. She also felt that her worrying kept everyone in her family 'safe'. So it never occurred to her to adjust this thinking and see if this actually made life better for her.

Take note of what was said about Jenny's attitude to worry – if we *believe* that worrying helps, then we will carry on doing it. So chipping away at this belief is the first step. Look again at Chapter 9 on beliefs and use the tools there to adjust this belief from, say, 'Worrying is helpful' to something like 'Worrying is hard to stop but rarely serves much useful purpose'.

Then you can start identifying and challenging the unhelpful thoughts that your 'worry' belief brings with it. Are they really true? If so, are any dire consequences going to be as dreadful as you think they might be? Are you underestimating your coping skills? Again, you will find the techniques for achieving this change earlier in the book so refer back to them if you need to.

LIVING WITH UNCERTAINTY

One of our beliefs about worry can be that the more we worry about something, the more likely we are to find that elusive 100 per cent certainty that all will be well without which we feel we cannot rest. However, 100 per cent certainty is very rare in life, and beginning to consider this is a helpful start.

Try it now

Think of all the areas of life in which you do tolerate uncertainty; for example, every time you get into a car, you could be involved in a major car accident. But that lack of certainty doesn't prevent you from driving off. Why is this? It is because in most areas of our lives we work with possibilities and probabilities rather than certainties. We accept that it's *possible* we might have a car accident, but we climb into the car anyway in the knowledge that we *probably* won't.

FACING YOUR FEAR

Don't create excuses for avoiding things that worry you. Move from 'What if... happens?' to 'If it does happen, I'll deal with it as best I can'. When facing up to worries, distraction can be very useful. Instead of sitting in the railway carriage hoping that there won't be an accident or that your claustrophobia won't overcome you, try counting how many back gardens have a child's trampoline in them, or how many thatched roofs you can see. If you find this helpful, ask yourself why? The answer will be that anxiety diminishes when we are not focusing on it all the time: a useful piece of information to have.

Phobic anxiety

A phobia is an anxiety focused on a very specific thing. The strange thing about phobias is that they are different for everyone. Some people can't bear spiders (arachnophobia), while others fear heights (acrophobia), blood (haemophobia) or being shut in a confined space (claustrophobia). There is a wide variety of other things that seem baffling to a non-phobic but frightening beyond belief to the sufferer.

Behavioural therapy is the most highly regarded treatment for phobia. Graded exposure is ideal, as the goal is to achieve gradual desensitization to the object of fear. Some people prefer to start with imaginal exposure to the situation and once they are comfortable with this, they move on to something more challenging.

If you suffer from phobia(s), refer back to the section in Chapter 8 that deals with graded exposure. However, if your phobic anxiety is extreme, then professional help is worth seeking.

Remember this

We are not looking for a quick fix way to reduce your anxiety. What we want is to help you learn to *tolerate* anxiety and see it gradually drift away on its own. Then the object you fear will no longer frighten you.

A PHOBIC EXAMPLE

Imagine you went to see a phobia expert to help you get over your fear of spiders. Once you had explained it to him, he said that he had just the cure. Reaching behind him he produced a large jar of spiders which he began to open in front of you.

Q What happens to your anxiety?

A It goes sky high!

When the expert notices this, he puts the lid back on the jar of spiders and puts it out of sight, apologizing for having caused you such distress.

Q What happens to your anxiety?

A It goes back down to normal

What a relief! But was it? Here is another question:

Q How far has this helped you to get over your fear of spiders?

A Not at all.

Now let's look at a more productive way of getting over phobias.

Key idea

Graded exposure can be adjusted and modified to suit you. Become comfortable with one step before you move on to another.

Incidentally, there's nothing to stop you simply going along to a clown party – research shows that it would be just as effective. However, that is not the easiest effort to make, and most people prefer the staggered approach.

Panic

Panic is a very common form of anxiety and many people can tell you of panic attacks that they have suffered. Often, panic is linked to claustrophobia (fear of confined spaces) as the sufferer feels threatened by being 'trapped' in a space or situation they cannot remove themselves from, and this increases their anxiety levels.

That is exactly what panic is – extreme anxiety, in which the physical symptoms become so marked and frightening that the person misinterprets these sensations and believes some harm is going to come to them, or that they are going to lose control completely.

Many people ask me how panic attacks start, where they come from? They find that the first attack occurs seemingly out of nowhere and from then on there is always the worry, if not the reality, of another one occurring.

A panic attack really is 'nothing' and can start from the smallest trigger, perhaps hearing an unexpected noise when alone in the dark, or feeling your heart miss a beat or palpitate for no apparent reason.

▶ Any small thing that sets up an anxiety signal from the brain to the body can then gather a momentum of its own with the anxiety suggesting further proof that something is wrong.

▶ The worry that something might be wrong increases the physical symptoms of anxiety, so that you are now worried not only that something is wrong but also about your physical reaction – are you going to have a heart attack because of this?

▶ The anxiety increases even further with these thoughts and the anxiety spiral is set in motion. It continues upwards until the physical sensations are so wretched that you will feel you cannot tolerate it and must take action, usually in the form of some sort of escape from the situation.

▶ Symptom relief leads to eventual subsidence of the anxiety so you feel that you did the right thing.

…but did you?

Key idea

What causes the anxiety to rise to 'can't stand it' levels is misinterpreting the physical symptoms as being harmful. This triggers the 'I must act' response of escape in order to reduce the possibility of serious harm – heart attack, serious illness – which the sufferer believes to be a fact rather than a misinterpretation.

The problem with panic attacks is that, once someone has had one, their fear of having another one is based not on being in a 'dangerous' situation again but simply on the memory of how physically unpleasant the experience was and a desire to avoid a repetition of it. Preventing another attack becomes all-important. Thus, if the panic attack happened in a confined space, all confined spaces are now to be avoided. If it happened in a restaurant, eating out becomes a no-no. The answer to prevent another panic attack seems to be avoidance, and it works very well. The problem is, however, that it *maintains* the fear. The person does not learn that, had they not fled the scene but waited out the panic attack, nothing would have happened and it would have died away of its own accord. However, that approach sounds like a risk and, understandably, who is going to wait around to test it out?

So the first 'next step' is to do some cognitive work and look for a less threatening alternative explanation for the feelings created by the panic attack – for example, recognizing that they are due to anxiety, which is not harmful, rather than to impending heart failure, which is.

Draw up a Thought Record and record your worst-case fears. Now jot down a less threatening alternative. For example: 'If I have a panic attack while driving I could die' might be replaced by 'I accept that driving always carries a small risk, but the likelihood of this happening is small while the cost to me of not driving is great'.

PREDICTION TESTING

As with phobias, graded exposure usually works best in dealing with panic. For example, if a person thinks they will have a panic attack if they get into a lift:

▶ A good first step might be to stand near the lift doors for a while, watching other people going in and out. The initial high anxiety will gradually reduce. They keep doing this until it becomes quite boring and they feel no further anxiety.

▶ A second step might be to wait for a quiet time, summon the lift and stand inside with the 'doors open' button pressed. Again, the high anxiety will eventually reduce.

▶ A third step could be to travel just one floor up or down in the lift, and so on, until the anxiety disappears.

▶ As always, if the anxiety is very high, imaginal exposure can be a good way to start.

You understand the process by now. You keep facing the fear but in graded steps, becoming comfortable with each one before moving on.

Remember this

A panic attack will never harm you in any way. Wait long enough and the anxiety will always subside. Stand up to it, it cannot hurt you.

Only by saying, 'bring it on' can you lose your fear of it.

Once you are no longer frightened, you will be unable to have another panic attack. Be brave. Never use avoidance or escape.

Social anxiety

Social anxiety is suffered by many people for much of the time. It is hard for anyone, however confident they may feel they are, to walk alone into a room full of strangers and not feel nervous. So imagine what it must be like if you are not confident; if you are rather shy by nature and don't have especially strong self-esteem? It can be so debilitating that some people close their lives down rather than put themselves into such anxiety-provoking situations; again, avoidance seems to them to be the 'cure'.

The fear particular to social anxiety is that of being judged harshly by others, of behaving in an unintentionally inappropriate way and of being humiliated in front of others.

Again, the fear is related to predictions rather than facts. (If I knew these fears were fact, I would never go out again and I don't suppose you would either!). The sufferer may not do anything that is embarrassing but they may feel that they have done so, or they fear that if they expose themselves to the scrutiny of others, then humiliation and disaster will follow. Over time the person will increasingly focus their attention on their social failings, making negative self-valuations and comparing themselves unfavourably to others. Avoidance does seem to be the sad solution adopted by many people with this anxiety problem.

Clients I work with tend to fall into two categories.

1 They openly admit to rarely going anywhere, and yet feel sadly isolated and even more of an 'outsider' because they don't. One of my clients turned down every invitation from her friends because of her social anxiety but felt unlovable when she told me that her friends 'didn't bother with her any more' and her self-esteem dropped even lower. This is another problem of social anxiety. It becomes a self-fulfilling prophecy and leads to even further isolation and feelings of worthlessness.

2 There are people who say, 'Oh, but I do go out. I always accept invitations but it still never gets any better'. The problem for these people is that, when questioned, I find that

they are still enacting safety behaviours without realizing it. They may go to the party but they will stand in a corner and fail to make eye contact. On the one hand, this keeps them safe, but on the other hand it reconfirms their 'I'm so dull nobody talked to me all evening' belief. Or they may leave the party early, refuelling their 'These things are awful and I'm just no good at small talk' belief. Either way, they are maintaining their social anxiety and confirming their fears that they are unable to interact socially with others in the normal way that they (often wrongfully) believe everyone else does.

GETTING OVER IT

One of the problems of social anxiety is that it is a self-fulfilling prophecy. When a nervous person walks into a room full of people, their thoughts tend to turn in on themselves as they try to imagine the impression they are making. They will start to wonder 'How do I look?', 'Am I coming across as boring?', 'Does this person feel that they cannot get away from me?', 'How will I cope with a gap in the conversation?', and so on. Their brain is in chatterbox mode with all these imaginings, and so their mind is not then fully focused on the person they are talking to. They will seem (as they are) pre-occupied and may not properly contribute to the conversation. Part of the person's mind is listening, while another part is feeding themselves negative self-talk.

The solution is not difficult and it works well for most people. You stop trying to make conversation and you become an 'active listener'. People worry so much about being a good conversationalist and you don't need to be! Just be a good listener and you will be loved by all. Most people are only too happy to talk about themselves if you give them an opportunity. It is such a simple skill and so easy to do. If you focus completely on what someone else is saying, you forget your own concerns. An easy trick, if you worry that you will not cope with a lull in the conversation, is to pick a word from the last sentence that was spoken, and say 'Tell me more'; for example, 'Tell me more about South America – I've never been there' or 'Ski-ing – I've never tried that. Tell me more about it', and so on.

Other tips for coping with social occasions include the following.

▶ When you have plucked up the courage to attend a social or work-related event, don't say to yourself afterwards, 'Phew. Thank goodness that's over'. Ask yourself, 'What did I learn from it?', 'How did I do?', 'What could I do that would help me in a similar situation in the future?'.

▶ Ask yourself whether the outcome was better or worse than you had hoped. Were your predictions overly negative? How did you feel at the end of the event?

▶ Again, imaginal exposure can be helpful. In your mind, practise introductions; for example, 'Hello, I'm Anne – It's good to meet you'. Imagine ways of ending a conversation. This might be something like 'It's been nice talking to you. I'm just off to get a drink from the bar'. Picturing these situations in your mind is close to actually finding yourself in them and will give you a lot of confidence.

Obsessive compulsive disorder

Obsessive compulsive disorder (OCD) is a type of anxiety disorder – some of us worry more than others. There is a very fine line between reasonable concern and obsessive worry, and it is difficult to define the division exactly as it is different for everyone. If someone is fairly relaxed about their extra checking, hand-washing or lining things up in a particular order even when they know that others don't do these things, then they don't need help. These actions would simply be described as their idiosyncratic tendencies.

But if the obsessive worrying and/or ritualizing causes an individual a real problem – because it leeches hours out of a person's day, or keeps them perpetually anxious and unable to function properly, for example – then it needs treatment.

In OCD, there is always an obsession with a compulsion, and when a sufferer is asked why they complete such rituals they often say that they 'don't feel right' unless the ritual is performed. What does 'doesn't feel right' mean? It usually means that the person feels that they will remain anxious unless they perform this seemingly senseless act. And who would want to feel anxious if they could get rid of it by some tiny ritual? Makes sense. Except that what it does is *maintain* the problem. It teaches people that they can reduce their anxiety by ritualizing. So they go on doing it.

The key to overcoming OCD has nothing to do with reducing anxiety. It is to do with reducing the strength of the individual's erroneous *belief* that something bad will happen if they don't ritualize – even if this 'something bad' is simply 'I will feel anxious' (although it might be to prevent harm to a family member, for example). Most people's OCD is maintained by making this error, which seems a completely natural response to them. However, once the belief strength is reduced (though Cognitive Behavioural experimentation), the anxiety will reduce and disappear of its own accord.

Some people talk about having 'pure O', i.e. they have lots of obsessively worrying thoughts all the time about harm of some sort but they don't have any compulsions. In fact, this is a misnomer; the mere act of mental focusing, mulling the thoughts over, giving them credence ('If I think it, it must be meaningful') is the compulsion.

The way forward is to teach sufferers to turn off their conversation with the OCD and to refuse to get drawn into 'could it/couldn't it?' sagas. Easy to say, of course, but very hard for the sufferer to do. Think about taking your shoe off and licking the sole with your tongue. Would you find that easy? Most people don't. This feeling is exactly how a person with OCD feels when, for example, they touch a light switch or a door handle. It is this enormously high anxiety 'in the moment' that causes them to be unable to function normally and to use avoidance, escape or reassurance to diminish their worries. Therapists have to teach sufferers to begin to risk a little and to tolerate anxiety and uncertainty in order to learn that no harm will come to them or their loved ones.

Sufferers always want to understand why they have this particular disorder. Is it genetic? Will their children get it? Why them? The present answer, frustratingly, is that no one knows for sure and, although much research is being done, there isn't a definitive answer. What we do know is that OCD is triggered or worsened by trauma. Most sufferers can trace the origins of their problem to some kind of traumatic event, after which the obsessions and compulsion either began or became more noticeable. It is also common for the symptoms to start early in life. Once the symptoms become more marked and an individual is diagnosed with the disorder, they can usually look back to regular rituals they performed in their childhood (perhaps as simple as always having to get out of bed on the same side) that they felt kept them 'safe'.

The main features of OCD are persistent, repetitive and disturbing thoughts which cause high anxiety when the sufferer ascribes meaning to such thoughts. Once the thought has meaning ('If I have thought about this, then I might do it', for example), the anxiety becomes extremely intense and the sufferer feels they need to find a way to reduce it. To do this, they will use a variety of safety behaviours, such as avoidance, reassurance seeking and/or performing rituals which might be mental (for example, repeated counting) or physical (for example, checking).

OCD is often described as an over-developed sense of responsibility, so that a conscientious concern for the well-being of others takes on problematic proportions. Many sufferers are also very ashamed of the content of their thoughts, which can sometimes be of a sexual, blasphemous or harming nature. There is no need – these thoughts are far more common than is often realized.

OCD is like a blackmailer without any photographs. If you are willing to call its bluff with a 'publish and be damned' attitude, you will find that it has nothing at all with which to harm you. OCD is all puff and wind – only good for two things:

1 making you highly anxious.

2 leeching a great deal of your time by engaging you in pointless conversations of the 'is it/isn't it?', 'could it/couldn't it?' kind that get no one anywhere.

If it is any consolation, the profile of characteristics of someone with OCD is that of the kindest, most thoughtful and conscientious person. You are the sort of person someone would give a newborn baby to knowing that it would be treated well. You are the person we would trust most to ensure that doors were locked, keys were safe, everyone was secure. Your great qualities simply have the downside of your being *too* responsible. You worry about things the rest of us don't care tuppence about. Can you imagine a burglar or a molester lying in bed at night *worrying* that they might be going to do something bad? Of course not. What does this tell you about yourself? You simply have a worry problem. Nothing else.

Negative predictions made by those with OCD can be:

▶ very specific; for example, 'Unless I ensure that every spoon in my kitchen is laid face downwards then my mother will die'

▶ quite vague; for example, 'I just know that something bad will happen'

▶ derived from fear of a supernatural being; for example, 'The Devil will cause something dreadful to happen'.

People have a very wide variety of obsessional worries. Sometimes people feel embarrassed to admit their own worries as they feel they will be judged harshly for having such thoughts. The reality is that OCD comes up with whatever is most important to you and reverses it. So the most conscientious mother will be the one to worry that she may harm her children; the most religious man will be afraid that he is going to shout out blasphemous thoughts in the street.

The most common obsessional worries concern:

► contamination

► causing unintentional harm to others

► checking

► sexual worries, including paedophilia.

SAFETY BEHAVIOURS USED WITH OCD

As with other anxiety disorders, the safety behaviours adopted maintain the problem, and strengthen its hold. These include:

► **Rituals.** These are the actions OCD tells us we must take to prevent catastrophe. They can be physical (lining up pens, checking the gas taps, relentlessly scrubbing hands or work surfaces, for example) or mental (such as going over and over specific rhymes or mantras or counting in specific sequences).

► **Reassurance seeking.** We seek an outsider's reassurance that the OCD thoughts are nonsense, or we ask them to do the checking/counting, etc. for us – 'just to be certain'. Other reassurance seeking can involve searching the internet for articles to prove/disprove what we are concerned about, and some sufferers can spend hours each day in this pointless activity.

► **Avoidance** of situations that might trigger obsessional worries. For example, if you worry that you might harm a child, you would walk around the park rather than going through it, in order to avoid the play area full of children 'just in case'.

GETTING OVER OCD

Until recently, the gold standard in treatment of OCD was a behavioural therapy called exposure and response prevention. This is still the cornerstone of beating OCD but some work on thought processes has also been shown to be helpful.

Exposure and response prevention is probably self-evident as a technique. We have worked earlier in the book with graded exposure as a behavioural strategy, and exposure and response prevention is the same. It requires the sufferer to expose themselves (in a structured and graded way) to the irrational fear and to resist engaging in the usual ritualistic safety behaviour. This can be achieved by gradually increasing the time delay before ritualizing until the level of anxiety reduces and the ritual becomes unnecessary, or by reducing the length of time that the ritual takes on a consistent basis, until a feeling of 'normality' is reached.

As well as exposure and response prevention, sufferers are asked not to seek reassurance from friends and family. This can be difficult for all concerned. Not only does it seem good sense to, say, reduce a sufferer's contamination anxiety levels by assuring them that you *did* wash your hands several times before touching the kitchen work surface, but it also makes life easier for the 'reassurer'. However, this is collusion with the OCD. The only reassurance a family member should give is to remind the enquirer that this is 'just OCD' and that they don't need reassurance. The OCD doesn't deserve more credit.

REDUCING THE MEANING OF OCD THOUGHTS

It cannot be emphasized strongly enough that OCD thoughts are meaningless nonsense. Don't fight them. Let the thoughts come. They are not harmful. Trying to fight them or banish them will only cause them to multiply. Try *not* thinking of pink balloons for a minute and you will see thousands of them. You cannot block your thoughts.

Key idea

The biggest driver of OCD is its relentless whispering to you that 'if you don't act, and something bad happens, then it will be all your fault'. There is no 100 per cent guarantee that something bad will/will not happen if you omit your ritual. But there is a good guarantee that, even if the feared event does/does not happen, your ritualizing or lack of it will have had no part in causing the outcome. So overcoming OCD is not about getting rid of the thoughts per se; it is about reducing the meaning to you of those thoughts. Does this make sense to you? I cannot reassure you that your partner won't get sick, but I can be certain that you cannot influence whether this happens or not with any particular ritual that you do or do not perform.

Your goal is to reduce the *meaning* of the thoughts so that it doesn't matter whether the thoughts are there or not. Once it doesn't matter, the thoughts will drift off of their own accord.

Here are some suggestions to help with this.

▶ Think of nothing but the obsessive thoughts for a defined time period – say one hour. If your thoughts wander, then bring them back to the obsessive thoughts. Eventually, you will become bored with these thoughts and see that there are better things to do with your day.

▶ Refuse to have any sort of conversation with the OCD. Don't even get into a rebuttal of what it is telling you – that would be 'hooking you in' and a victory. Simply say something along the lines of 'Be that as it may… I'm off to make lunch now', or whatever. Don't talk to it – at all.

▶ Label the thoughts. Tell yourself 'These are just my OCD thoughts; they are complete time-wasters and don't deserve a moment of my attention'.

OCD is incapable of causing harm or of persuading you to cause harm. However, it is very persuasive on this. Look back to Chapter 14 and use the 'Theory A (danger) versus Theory B (worry)' technique described there to overcome these concerns.

Use the thought-challenging skills described in early chapters to challenge such beliefs as 'Thinking something can make it happen' or 'I must take full responsibility for the safety of others' or 'Just thinking about it is as bad a doing it'.

OCD is very good at bringing doubt into things. It will suggest, 'Are you really sure that this is an OCD thought?', 'Are you really certain that you can risk that?', and so on. When in doubt, treat the thought as OCD and use the same skills and techniques on it as you do for all your other thoughts. But more importantly, to overcome OCD you must:

▶ learn to live with uncertainty and doubt; we cannot ever achieve 100 per cent certainty so stop seeking it. Learn to live with 'probabilities', which is fine.

- learn to tolerate anxiety. As with other anxiety disorders, the mistake that sufferers make is to focus on anxiety reduction. Even at its highest and most potent, *anxiety cannot harm you*. Instead, focus on *reducing the strength of the erroneous belief*. Then your anxiety will die away of its own accord.

- learn to accept risk. We must all risk a little and we do. Every time you drive down the road you are taking a risk. When you walk down the street, get on a plane, turn on the cooker. There is a tiny element of risk inherent in almost any activity. Your rational brain is happy to take these small risks. Don't let your OCD tell you that you cannot accept risk, that you must have 100 per cent certainty. This is impossible; if you believe it, you will stop doing anything. Risk a little, live a little. All will be fine.

OCD can seem an especially worrying problem and hard to overcome. But I beg you to work at it and use the skills described in this book to defeat it. Working to defeat OCD can be hard – I do appreciate and understand this – but the alternative, living with it forever, is surely even harder? Kick it into touch. You can. Really.

Health anxiety

People find health anxiety very hard to live with. In some cases the sufferer is almost totally consumed with worry about being seriously ill, to the point that it causes serious distress not only to them personally but also to their families and work colleagues. Constant reassurance is time-consuming, especially as this cannot always be given. And even when it is, evidence of good health is disbelieved and the individual remains convinced that they are seriously ill.

As with other anxiety disorders, the sufferer's desire to reduce this terrible anxiety causes them to use safety behaviours that in fact maintain it. These safety behaviours include

- reassurance seeking – turning up again and again at the doctor's with the same worries

- scanning for symptoms – constantly self-checking for symptoms and using external sources such as the reference library or the internet to seek out symptom descriptions. Use of the internet can further fuel the anxiety as it will often provide additional symptoms that the sufferer had not previously considered. This in turn leads to even further worries as the sufferer tries to interpret and re-interpret what these could mean.

▷ failure to accept any evidence that might suggest there is nothing wrong.

Constantly focusing on the physical symptoms to see if they have changed in any way causes extreme anxiety – and, as you now know well, anxiety has its own adverse physical symptoms, which result in even more 'evidence' that all is not well.

The sufferer's lack of belief when evidence is placed before them by medical practitioners is a cause for concern. Often, sufferers will feel that the doctor 'got it wrong' somehow, or that perhaps a different doctor would have noticed different symptoms. People who worry about infections such as AIDS insist on being checked but when tests come back clear, it gives rise to the new worry that perhaps they didn't have it prior to the test but might have now if the needle wasn't properly sterilized. In other words, there is no reassurance that can adequately quell health anxiety as it is exactly that: anxiety. And you understand well now that we treat anxiety quite differently to this.

GETTING OVER IT

First, it is helpful to know how the individual thinks. For example, one person might hold the view that 'If I maintain a vigilance for the signs and symptoms of illness, I will be OK', while another person might think, 'Just thinking about my illness will bring it on'.

Belief testing, as you have learned in earlier chapters, is very helpful. 'Where is the evidence?' is always the best question we can ask, using a 'for' and 'against' list to help chip away at negative beliefs. For example:

▷ Evidence for serious illness might include: having pain in, for example, one's leg on a regular basis; plus further 'back up' evidence of feeling tired and lethargic. Perhaps a recent newspaper article about someone who died whose symptoms sounded similar might also be considered as 'evidence for'.

▶ Evidence against might consist of: having had medical checks both with a GP and a specialist, neither of whom found anything wrong; noticing that when you are pre-occupied you sometimes forget your symptoms and they seem to go away; appreciating that anxiety can bring its own aches and pains; and accepting that, in spite of all this worry, your body appears to be working well.

As well as assessing the evidence for and against, conducting a survey of friends and family can be a positive help. This can be done very informally, just by asking, 'Do you ever get... [describe your own concern]... and have you done anything about it?'. Collating the responses of others, which will probably be very varied, may give a more balanced view that others don't see such aches and pains as especially threatening, that they go away on their own, etc.

Reducing safety behaviours, such as turning up for endless medical tests and searching through medical books and the internet, is also very important.

As ever, using a Thought Record to notice negative interpretations and to find less threatening alternatives to the worries will be very helpful.

Focus points

∗ There is a range of specific anxiety disorders that many people suffer from. They are common, they cause no harm except in the time and energy wasted on them, and they can all be overcome with application.

∗ If you don't have any of these difficulties yourself, remember that many people you know may struggle with one or more of them, and you will now have far more empathy and understanding of their problems.

∗ If you suffer seriously from any of the disorders mentioned here, I would stress that this has been only a brief overview and you may need to obtain extra help for yourself, at least initially, by reading more in-depth books on the specific problem that you have and possibly considering some professional help. Also, if you have reason to be especially interested in any specific disorder, undertake further research and reading to increase your knowledge of the full range of treatments available.

* CBT offers specific treatment protocols for each anxiety disorder, rather than a general 'one size fits all' model. So you need to learn and understand the different skills required, depending on the disorder identified.
* I haven't asked you to rate your exercise efforts in this last chapter as we have been describing very specific problems here that you may not personally suffer from. This chapter (and Chapter 14) have been of a more informative nature for you. If you do recognize your own problems in these pages and those problems are severe in nature, then specialist books and/or specific professional help will be your best way forward.

Your final step

Your final step will depend very much on why you read this book. If it was curiosity – you felt you would like to know more about CBT – then I hope that the book has enlightened you a little. If you felt that you have a few problems you might like some help with, I hope this book has given you some new skills and techniques to try and that it has also been easy to follow and understand. Consistency will help you to succeed. Don't run at it at a pace you can't keep up. As suggested at the beginning, make a plan and stick with it, and you will eventually see results. If you read this book thinking that you might possibly undertake some CBT training, then I hope I have convinced you that it is a great therapy and that you do continue with it.

In any event, thank you for reading the book and I hope that, each in your different ways, you will have taken something from it that you intend to use in the future.

Useful resources

Anxiety UK
Helpline: 08444 775 774
Website: www.anxietyuk.org

British Association for Behavioural and Cognitive Psychotherapies
Imperial House, Hornby Street, Bury BL9 5BN
Tel: 0161 705 4304
Email: babcp@babcp.com
Website: www.babcp.org.uk

British Association for Counselling and Psychotherapy
BACP House, 15 St John's Business Park, Lutterworth LE17 4HB
Tel: 01455 883300
Email: bacp@bacp.co.uk
Website: www.bacp.co.uk

British Psychological Society
St Andrews House, 48 Princess Road East, Leicester LE1 7DR
Tel: 0116 254 9568
Email: enquiries@bps.org.uk
Website: www.bps.org.uk

Depression Alliance
Tel: 0845 123 23 20
Website: www.depressionalliance.org

Oxford Cognitive Therapy Centre
Warneford Hospital, Oxford OX3 7JX
Tel: 01865 7388166
Email: octc@obmh.nhs.uk
Website: www.octc.co.uk

Oxford Mindfulness Centre, Powic Building, University of
Oxford Department of Psychiatry, Warneford Hospital, Oxford
OX3 7JX
Tel: 01865 613144
Website: www.oxfordmindfulness.org

Mindfulness-based stress reduction
www.mindfree.co.uk
www.bemindful.co.uk

USA

Beck Institute for Cognitive Therapy and Research
One Belmont Avenue, Suite 700, Bala Cynwyd, PA 19004-1610
Tel: 610 664 3020
Email: beckinst@gim.net
Website: www.beckinstitute.org

Center for Cognitive Therapy
PO Box 5308, Huntington Beach, CA 92615-5308
Tel: 714 963 0528
Email: mooney@padesky.com
Website: www.MindoverMood.com

Center for Mindfulness
University of Massachusetts Medical School, 55 Lake Avenue
North, Worcester, MA 01655
Tel: 508 856 2656
Email: mindfulness@umassmed.edu
Website: www.umassmed.edu

Cognitive Therapy Center of New York
137 East 36th Street, Suite #4, New York, NY 10016
Tel: 212 686 6886
Email: ocdzone@ocdonline.com
Website: www.cognitivebehavioralcenter.com

To contact the author:
Email: chrissyw2@aol.com
Website: www.christinewildingcbt.co.uk

Here is a small, broad-based selection of the many books that
might be helpful to you.

Beck, J. S. (1995). Cognitive Therapy: The Basics and Beyond.
New York: Guilford Press.

Clark, D. & Fairburn, C. (1997). Science and Practice of
Cognitive Behavioural Therapy. Oxford: Oxford University
Press.

Covey, S. (2004). The 7 Habits of Highly Effective People. London: Simon & Schuster.

Gilbert, P. (2000). Overcoming Depression. London: Robinson.

Greenberger, D. & Padesky, C. A. (1995). Mind over Mood: Change the Way You Feel by Changing the Way You Think. New York: Guilford Press.

Jeffers, S. (2007). Feel the Fear and Do It Anyway: 20th Anniversary Edition. London: Random House.

Kennerley, H. (2009). Overcoming Anxiety. London: Robinson.

Leahy, R. (2003). Cognitive Therapy Techniques. New York, Guilford Press.

Salkovskis, P. (Ed.) (1996). Frontiers of Cognitive Therapy. New York: Guilford Press.

Tolle, E. (2001). The Power of Now. London: Hodder & Stoughton.

Wells, A. (1997). Cognitive Therapy of Anxiety Disorders: A Practice Manual and Conceptual Guide. Chichester: Wiley.

Westbrook, D., Kennerley, H. & Kirk, J. (2011). An Introduction to Cognitive Behaviour Therapy: Skills and Applications. London: Sage.

Williams, J. M. G. (1992). The Psychological Treatment of Depression: A Guide to the Theory and Practice of Cognitive Behaviour Therapy (Second ed.). London: Routledge.

Williams, M. & Penman, D. (2011). Mindfulness: A Practical Guide to Finding Peace in a Frantic World. London: Piatkus.

Williams, M., Teasdale, J., Segal, Z. & Kabat-Zinn, J. (2007). The Mindful Way Through Depression. New York: Guilford Press.

Wills, F. & Sanders, D. (1977). Cognitive Therapy: Transforming the Image. London: Sage.

Index